A World After Its Own Image

Ben Stahnke

Pravda Media

Pravda Media

Copyright © 2017 by Ben Stahnke
Published by Pravda Media 2017

First Printing: 2017

ISBN-13: 978-1981982585
ISBN-10: 1981982582

Pravda Media
3180 W Greenwood St Box 28
Springfield, MO 65807

www.pravda-m.com

Ordering Information: Special discounts are available on quantity purchases by corporations, associations, educators, and others. For details, contact the publisher at the above listed address. U.S. trade bookstores and wholesalers: Please contact Pravda Media Tel: (417) 374-1966; or email at outreach@pravda-m.com

ACKNOWLEDGEMENTS

The present work is dedicated to my beloved mentor, thesis advisor, and friend, the great Dr. Scott Warren, who sadly passed away during the completion of the present work. Without your Socratic guidance, Scott, I would not be who I am.

I also dedicate this work to my close friend Nathan Bennett, who sadly took his own life during the writing of this thesis. Life is fleeting; we are often left without chances to say goodbye.

"We call communism the real movement which
abolishes the present state of things."

Karl Marx & Friedrich Engels

Table of Contents

CHAPTER I

Introduction

Land Relations and Landownership

"The *right of landownership*," wrote a young Karl Marx, "has its source in robbery" ("Early Writings" 103). This robbery, we might speculate, has existed since time immemorial. Indeed, history itself might be conceived as a series of unending robberies; lapping waves of violent displacement. We might imagine that these waves of displacement, unending cycles of taking and taking-back, are natural. And indeed, we can begin from this hypothesis: land is held through a natural violence, or a threat of violence. When one becomes incapable of holding on to a space of land, another, stronger, comes in to take ownership. Violence, in the case of the domination of land, can take both material and ideological form. The threat of physical violence, an idea of violence, is often enough for an individual, or a social class, to maintain land holdings.

What happens to an individual—families of individuals, or cultures of individuals—who dwell in a place for years, hundreds or thousands of years, even? It might safely be assumed that a specific land-relationship develops which influences not only the individual, but her material efforts and her resultant cultural practices as well. On this idea, Marx and Engels wrote, "As individuals express their life, so they are. What they are, therefore, coincides with their production, both with *what* they produce and *how* they produce it" ("The German Ideology" 7). In other words, the land shapes both product ad producer. Following this, we can safely assert the first premise of our argument: individuals, and groups of individuals, possess a productive material-psychological relationship with the land upon which they dwell. This can be asserted without any great leaps in logic. Foregoing some traumatic split, for example, individuals tend to dwell fondly upon memories of hometowns, local parks, forests, and beaches. And amidst mobile peoples—peripatetic labor forces moving from place to place in search of employment—the hometown might be seen as a locus of memorial fondness.

Over time, we can imagine, the *ways* in which lands are occupied, cultivated, and utilized for sustenance might tend to coalesce around a material status quo, thus becoming, simply, *the ways by which things happen.* However, the relationship of human-to-land is always mediated, in society itself, by relationships of social power. Dominating social classes emerge to control the *best* portions of land, and states quickly evolve to codify class rule. In *The State and Revolution*, Lenin wrote that, "The state is the product and the manifestation of the *irreconcilability* of class antagonisms. The state arises when, where and to the extent that class antagonisms *cannot* be objectively reconciled" (273). Antagonisms between social groups—social classes—themselves concern resource and land access, and revolve around ideas of public power. This public power, Engels wrote, "exists in every state; it consists not merely of armed men, but of material appendages, prisons and coercive institutions of all kinds" (qtd. in Lenin 275). Here, coercion implies *threat of repression*, or the *idea* of violence. In our view, this idea revolves around, and emerges from, man's relationship to land itself.

What then is the nature of this relationship, of this bond? If we remain consistent with the lens of historical materialism—acknowledging the import of material relations, of individuals producing and reproducing the necessary means of human species-existence—we might then hold that a fondness for a specific plot of land is bound up within a material necessity for life itself. The land provides both shelter and food, and without it human society, humans themselves, would cease to exist. The existence of all species of life, *Homo sapiens* notwithstanding, entails a necessary relationship to some type of life-supportive environment. Individuals are drawn to land, specific pieces of land, out of the necessity for the basic requirements of sustenance and reproduction. This should be fairly easy to accept. Fondness for one specific piece of land over others might also be seen both as anecdotal and accidental: we are drawn to the land which has historically sustained us, our forebears, and their children. The land, however, tends to be conceptualized as an "other": an alien thing which seems to exert power over man himself. We are, by virtue of the locus of our perspective, ourselves and not the land. But, to posit this stark contrast between the individual and the land does not do justice to the intrinsic *unitive* relationship between species and environment. The former may not exist without the latter. Indeed, the former essentially *emerges* from the latter. So, here we are led to a vision of species/environment—human/land—relations which might be conceived as *identical*, yet tensioned; sublated and synthetic. In a word: dialectical. Man identifies with the land, and is in turn shaped by it. To borrow, yet reassign, a few words from Marx, both man and land "are indeed distinct but they also form a unity" ("Early Writings" 158). We shall return to this idea of distinction/unity throughout the following pages.

Following our first premise—that individuals possess a productive mental-psychological relationship with the land upon which they dwell—we arrive now at our second premise: in our present epoch, individuals are increasingly alienated from the land upon which they dwell; the life-supportive mental-psychological relationship with the land itself has been extremely weakened, if not shattered altogether. Marx wrote that, "man's relation to nature is directly his relation to man, and his relation to man is directly his relation to nature, to his own natural function" ("Early Writings" 154). Following this, we might conceptualize land-relations—and land-alienation—historically: land relations mirror *social* relations which, at their root, are influenced by *economic* relations. And thus land relations can be seen to ultimately mirror economic relations. The driving economic force in whichever epoch of history man finds himself is thus the template for his relationship with the land. "[S]ocial organization [evolves] directly out of production and commerce, which in all ages forms the basis of the State and of the rest of the idealistic superstructure" ("The German Ideology" 27). But, here we must make several distinctions. On the one hand, we have the individual's relationship with the land as molded by the epochal template of social history. Feudal land relations helped to shape a specific mental-psychological relationship of the individual to her environment. Capitalist land relations help to shape another. But, on the other hand, we have the fact that land relations derive from the material reality of the production and reproduction of human existence, thus forming a sort of species-specific (we might say intrinsic) necessity. Land relations are thus endemic to human existence itself.

We now arrive at the conclusion to our syllogism, a key problematic which follows quite naturally from the previous two premises: if individuals have a necessary mental-psychological relationship with the land upon which they dwell, and—following that this relationship is shaped by the economic epoch in which humanity finds itself—if our present epoch shapes this relationship in such a way as to diminish this relationship almost entirely, we thus, as a species, find ourselves in a position where the diminishment of our land-relationship (as caused by the structuring of economic relations) becomes an existential problem for the species itself—an ideological death spiral where increasing alienation only creates further alienation; our future both bleak and uncertain, and our extinction, by way of a lost land-relationship, a very real possibility.

Our conclusion helps us to arrive at the central issue around which the present work is situated: under the epoch of capitalism, the *epoch of the bourgeoisie*—the dominant social class in the capitalist era—the alienation endemic to present-day *bourgeois* human-land relations will, left unchecked, eventually lead to the utter ruin of not only our own species, but, following the environment-destructive practices of the capitalist mode of production (*produktionsweise*), to all species and to the planet itself. Should humanity ever seek to move beyond the destructive economic practices of the capitalist *produktionswiese*, the ways in which we, as a species, organize the social and economic relations entailed by our present mode of production *must* be addressed. Alternatives must be realized and accelerated. We must look to and address the *reproductive source* of alienative land relations.

Here, we must admit that we add nothing new to the collection of works comprising the great Marxist classics. Much of this has already been said by others, and far better, in regards to both political and revolutionary theory. However, if there is anything new in this presentation, it shall lie upon the *ideological-theoretical* structure of land relations themselves, differing in that our focus shall primarily lie upon the political, the ideological, and the ontological relationship of *man to land*, and upon the mechanism by which the endemic *alienation from nature* entailed by the capitalist mode of production reproduces itself. The following work is thus a work of both philosophy *and* political theory.

Our first chapter will take the form of a critique of bourgeois ideology itself—that mental enslavement which violates political justice and which legitimates a capitalism of exploitation and alienation. To do this, an historical lens must be adopted, and we shall attempt to both deconstruct and rearticulate a *philosophical* history of the bourgeoisies: one which moves bourgeois land relations out of the feudal era—the era of manors and hofs—and into the era of private property and the profit motive. We will discuss the influence of one early theorist—David Hume—and we will examine the ways in which his influence helped to shape the historical force of bourgeois ideology. And, we will attempt the show that the crafting of bourgeois ideology, of the land-alienation of the proletariat, has been both purposeful and strategized: a weaponized idea-structure. Following this, we will begin to conceptualize the history of

4

what Jürgen Habermas called the "bourgeois public sphere"—that culture of bourgeois class rule: once-European, now-global. We shall discuss how the now-global public sphere of the bourgeoisies has coopted human reason itself, and how it continues to produce and reproduce itself in the minds of its subjects as a legitimating ideology of control. We will conclude our first chapter with an examination of the primary ways in which bourgeois ideology is reproduced in the minds of the global proletariat and petty bourgeois alike: public education. We will make suggestions for a countering of this sort of reproduction via an oppositional education—a radical education which *must* accompany revolutionary praxis, if praxis itself is to succeed in a subversion of the capitalist mode of production.

Recalling our opening idea, that land is held by violence, our aim shall be to ultimately examine the mental violence by which the land is now presently held: ideological force and the *threat* of repressive force. We shall examine the ways in which the ideological and repressive force of the system of capitalism has become global through cooption and control: a now-unipolar world in which all land is held and controlled by a small class of moneyed *élite*—held with violence by a class which has become alien to its own species, a class which is in turn held in bondage by its own exploitative economy, "more enslaved under a power alien to them [...] the *world-market*" ("The German Ideology" 27).

Our second chapter will take the shape of an examination of the preconditions necessary for a contemporary building-up of a theory of *communist* land relations. We carefully avoid the articulation of such a theory itself, but only explore what need be in place to do so. Future works may indeed see the articulation of such a theory. We shall examine what we see as three main preconditions for the articulation of a theory of communist land relations: the necessity for such a theory to remain critical, the necessity for such a theory to remain political, and the necessity for such a theory to remain dialectical: a critical-political theory of land relations which itself acknowledges a type of tensioned metaphysical identicalism of subject and object, species-being and environment.

Marx himself noted that, "Communism as a fully developed naturalism is humanism and as a fully developed humanism is naturalism" ("Early Writings" 155). Following Marx, we maintain that the idea of communism—a communist *produktionsweise*—*is* an idea of naturalism. It is an eschatological idea which envisions humanity moving *forward* into an egalitarian, communitarian, and humanitarian future—one with both an advanced technological base and an (anti-) ideological resituation of the human animal back into its natural-world context. It is thus an idea which sees a species fulfilled. However, "Communism is not for us a stable state which is to be established, an *ideal* to which reality will have to adjust itself. We call communism the *real* movement which abolishes the preset state of things" ("The German Ideology" 26). We hold that communism is indeed inevitable: the logical result of a socialism which will, upon capitalism's self-collapse, ascend as the dominant mode of production. "The conditions of this movement result from the premises now in existence" ("The German Ideology" 26). The idea of communism, that idea which Alain Badiou called *the communist hypothesis,* entails its own unique theory of land relations—a theory which has yet to be fully articulated—and, in our view, seeks to *restore* humanity to the land, unalienating the individual from her alienated and isolated state, and restoring her to a position of world-immersion, where her mental-psychological relationship with the land is developed to its fullest; (wo)man thus existing as a species truly in harmony with her environment. The conclusion to the present work will thus pave the way for future works to better articulate oppositional land relations—contracapitalist environmental philosophies—which do not simply reproduce, a priori, the extant exploitative system, but which articulate species-relationships to the land that are reciprocally beneficial, sustainable, and socially egalitarian.

CHAPTER II

Bourgeois Land Relations: Ideological Mechanisms, Cooption, and Reproductivity

Held by Violence

Extant capitalist economic practice, protected by its host of corporative states—protectionist business structures which are at the same time multifarious and ubiquitous—is a human response to the world, to land itself. But what sort of response is it? It is one which, at its root, views the world as a set of resources to be harvested for profit. Resources which, in turn, are held and controlled by the violence of a dominant social class. This is the radix of capitalist environmental philosophy. And this idea dominates our life. It is apparent everywhere we look. The land itself does not belong to us for free travel, to do with as we please. There are no lands up for grabs without the violent upheaval of native populations. The earth is spoken for. And the earth, along with all of her resources, exists for profit by those who themselves own the earth: the neoliberal profiteers—the bourgeoisies who utilize a violence both ideological and material.

We may test this theory by conducting a simple thought experiment, attempting in our minds to imagine a large period of time spent inside one of any modern nation's national parks: wild spaces which, under capitalism, do not reflect the world-as-it-is, but rather the world-as-spectacle—a pristine geography cleansed of its indigenous habitation and now-safe for recreation. Our present day conception of "wilderness" itself arises from a bourgeois conception of land relations: a romanticized, de-populated "frontier"—nature as a type of semi-cultivated, yet semi-wild, recreational space (ranger stations, gift shops, and access roads notwithstanding). Rather than providing a window into that which the world once was most naturally—wild, free, and bountifully populated—we are presented with a bourgeois conception of "the wild." And to gain access to a portion of "wild" land, say one of these national parks, we can imagine that we are required to attain permits, to pay a fee, and to submit to the authority of the agents of the park—the rangers and park police. Under capitalism, even when we seek freedom in the wild spaces of the world, we must do so with *permission*, at our expense, and with strict obeisance to the presence of the agents of the repressive state apparatus. We seek freedom in the woods, yet even here we are profoundly unfree. And herein lies the conclusion of our thought experiment: even when we imagine ourselves going "back to the land," retreating into the woods and the wilds, we must do so under strict authority, in a controlled fashion, and through a conception of land which is ultimately epochal—and thus unreal. Under capitalism, all land is held with a type of violent control.

We explore this example to consider a point: land is controlled, held with a violence to which we must submit. Contrarily, there do exist spaces outside the national park structure—the national forest service lands, grasslands, and so on—where no fee is required, and where individuals might, for some time, evade notice. However, at its root, this land is also tightly controlled by agencies such as, in the U.S., the Department of the Interior, the U.S. Forest Service, and the various Departments of Natural Resources. Our point here is not to quibble over the fee total itself, or the length of time in which we might avoid detection, but rather to emphasize one key point: if an individual seeks immersion in the wilderness of their world, a most natural species-act, she must do so in recognition that the land in which she immerses herself does not, ultimately, belong to her. She may not take up residence, nor build a structure, nor extract resources for profit or use—those rights belong to only a few. And further, most tracts of federal and state wilderness have strictly-enforced limits on the amount of days one might spend within their boundaries. Activities are limited, and recreation alone is typically implied; residence, of course, is denied.

Further: in the U.S., where the stain of colonialism is most recent, when one is out in the wild spaces of the national parks, forests, and grasslands—e.g., Olympic National Park in Washington, Yellowstone National Park in Wyoming, or Rocky Mountain National Park in Colorado—the recognition soon dawns that the land upon which one stands is land which was attained, most recently, by violent conquest, by genocide, and by the brutal subjugation of indigenous populations. It should occur to us that, in the U.S., most national parks and state wilderness areas have historically, until the arrival of colonial Europeans—and prior to the genocide of the Native Americans—been *consistently* populated; only now do they exist as depopulated spectacles. The old sacred spaces, homelands, and burial mounds of the Native

Americans are now protected under capitalism as showpieces—museum exhibits for the residents of a business-minded settler state. The point we are trying to make here is this: under capitalism, in the U.S., the exploitative doctrine of private property is so total that every square inch of land has been both claimed and commodified—whether for private, state, or federal gain. And indeed, we also submit that the control of a nation's wildest areas—its mountains and deserts, river-ways and forests—under the staunch protection of police-trained, military-armed, and helicopter-equipped park rangers is also itself a military strategy for the bourgeoisies—our dominant social class. The bloody efforts of the U.S. Indian Wars provide such an example that remote spaces can oftentimes become holdouts of resistance.

We submit that the *land relations* in the U.S. rest, primarily, upon a triad of factors: repressive regulation (military control), economic regulation (forestry, mining and fracking in national forests; tourism in national parks), and ideological regulation (superstructural elements such as: the concept of landownership itself, private property, and the legal control of geographies). All three of these factors can be examined by one of two epistemological categories: utilizing either an ideological or a material lens. Indeed both categories are entailed by all three factors, but for the sake of the present work we shall turn our eye towards the former—towards the ideological conditions by which land is both controlled and exploited. Here, we arrive at our focus for this section, and indeed for the present work itself: the *ideological mechanism by which land is controlled*. Following Louis Althusser on the subject (73 – 78), we submit that the mechanism of land-control is situated as such—as an aspect of state control—that it contains both a physical and a *mental* element: a repressive appendage as well as an ideological appendage. It entails both a material and an immaterial element, however unified these two seemingly disparate concepts present themselves in reality.

In the following pages of the present chapter, we will attempt, overarchingly, to critique bourgeois land relations, to analyze their history, and to look to their modes of reproduction. We hold here that bourgeois land relations are *entailed* by bourgeois ideology: a geographically-focused sub-ideology of bourgeois economic-legitimation. We also hold that bourgeois land relations, as a function of the ideology of capitalism, form the foundational structure of capitalist environmental philosophy—a philosophy which, at its core, holds the earth itself to be a collection of resources to be harvested for profit; a philosophy which predicates upon the alienation of the human organism from its natural world context; a philosophy which both alienates and exploits, controls and profits. We also hold that any sort of oppositional environmentalism—*green capitalism*—which emerges from a base of such an environmental philosophy only presupposes, as a solution, the problem against which it seeks to operate; thus negating the efficacy of its efforts.

To critique bourgeois land relations, we will take the following approach. While not explicitly an historical treatise—our aim here is, in fact, philosophical—we shall as such begin by briefly recapitulating the history of what Jürgen Habermas called the "bourgeois public sphere": that realm of influence of the bourgeoisie class which now holds a type of cultural hegemony over all human life. Bourgeois ideology—the economically-supportive, class protectionist idea structure, within which bourgeois land relations rest—did not descend from the heavens, nor did it rise simply from the minds of Hume, Locke, Hobbes, Harrington, and others. No—it grew dialectically, both hand in hand and historically, from material, capitalist economic practice and from the capitalist mode of production. "[H]ere we ascend from earth to heaven. That is to say, we do not set out from what men say, imagine, conceive, nor from men as narrated, [...] We set out from real, active men, and [...] demonstrate the development of the ideological reflexes and echoes of this life-process" ("The German Ideology" 14). Following Marx and Engels' methodology, our aim here will be to shed a degree of light on such a history of this growth as *material* in nature, contra the idealistic (and ideological) ways in which man imagines himself moving historically.

Secondly, to paint a stronger picture of the development of bourgeois land relations, we shall critique the ideas of one such capitalist ideologue in particular: David Hume. We shall then explore how bourgeois ideology has emerged to subvert reason itself, and how such an ideology presents itself as a mechanism of control over civil society. We will then move on to an analysis of how bourgeois ideology is primarily reproduced. We hold that this happens primarily, and materially, via public education—what we are calling the *weaponized curriculum* of the bourgeoisies—and we will offer the idea that a critical, radical education might be used as an addendum to revolutionary praxis, helping to combat the reproduction of bourgeois ideology, and thus helping to also combat the spread of the alienating and exploitative structure of bourgeois land relations.

The Bourgeois Public Sphere

Jürgen Habermas once wrote that, the "bourgeois public sphere arose historically in conjunction with a society separated from the state" (127). He continued by elaborating that the bourgeois social sphere "could be constituted as its own sphere to the degree that on the one hand the reproduction of life took on private forms, while on the other hand the private realm as a whole assumed public relevance" (127). This relevance suggests a social power—the same *public power* of the bourgeoisies, upon which Engels commented when he wrote that, "Possessing the public power and the right to exact taxes, the officials now exist as organs of society standing above society. The free, voluntary respect which was accorded to the organs of the gentile organization does not satisfy them, even if they could have it" (qtd. in Lenin 277). The public power of the bourgeoisie class—their social power within the polis structure—is a phenomenon which can be examined both historically and philosophically. Our aim in this chapter shall be to do both.

Here, we arrive at a foundational, and operating, fact of bourgeois land relations. What we earlier posited as a primary doctrine of capitalist economy *and* capitalist environmental philosophy—the view that the earth exists as a collection of resources to be harvested for profit—has, as its root, a socio-ideological impetus; the social character of European mercantile culture. Bourgeois land relations take their root in the socio-public fabric of bourgeois culture itself. And, if we are to examine the concept of bourgeois land relations fully, we must first correctly conceptualize what is meant by the term *bourgeoisie* as a socioeconomic descriptor; we must look to the history of the bourgeoisie class. World-historically, our bourgeoisies arose from the town-dwellers and the merchants of the European feudal era—a protected class of the *ancien régime*. While far from homogenous, our bourgeoisies were yet unified by similar logics: a logic of accumulation and a logic of profit *über alles*. Marx and Engels noted that:

> The bourgeoisie, wherever it has got the upper hand, has put an end to all feudal, patriarchal, idyllic relations. It has pitilessly torn asunder the motley feudal ties that bound man to his "natural superiors," and has left no other bond between man and man than naked self-interest, than callous "cash payment." It has drowned the most heavenly ecstasies of religious fervor, of chivalrous enthusiasm, of philistine sentimentalism, in the icy water of egotistical calculation. It has resolved personal worth into

exchange value, and in place of the numberless indefeasible chartered freedoms, has set up that single, unconscionable freedom—Free Trade. In one word, for exploitation, veiled by religious and political illusions, it has substituted naked, shameless, direct, brutal exploitation ("The Communist Manifesto" 11).

Emergent as the villains, the slave-masters, and the world-dominators of our age, it might be easy to forget that the bourgeoisies have had a revolutionary history of their own: first as an oppressed burgher class with ties to the merchantry of feudal Europe, secondly as an armed insurgent class during the decline of the aristocracies, the waves of European revolutions, and the demise of feudal socioeconomy, and thirdly as the true lords of their new world: a moneyed *élite* in the technological wonderland of the Twentieth and Twenty-First centuries. Evidence of bourgeois class-rule is, everywhere, apparent. Corporate skyscrapers—dominating the skylines of the global metropoles—have replaced the cathedrals, manors, and castles of the prior feudal era. Armed forces of subservient police and military men—appendages of the repressive apparatus of the bourgeoisies—rampantly protect property rights and continue bloody wars of conquest: opening up ever-new markets, destroying and coopting oppositional populations, and creating ever-new labor forces in foreign lands—cracking the heads of those who would dare to resist the new world. By domination or by willing acceptance, few are the nations which would not now call themselves capitalist. "The ideas of the ruling class are in every epoch the ruling ideas: i.e. the class, which is the ruling material force of society, is at the same time its ruling intellectual force" ("The German Ideology" 39). The world today is truly a world after the mind of the bourgeoisie; a world after its own image. It is a world where social relations have deteriorated fully into callous monetary relationships, where a control of fiat currency equates to social power, and where the forces and materials of the natural world itself are naught but resources destined for profit—for the continual revolution of productive forces and products, and for the enrichment of but a small subsection of humanity. The world itself is controlled—sold back to the underclasses of civil society, who seem to have long since forgotten their relationship to it, mythical and wondrous as it once was. Georg Lukács noted that:

Bourgeoisie and proletariat are the only pure classes in bourgeois society. They are the only classes whose existence and development are entirely dependent on the course taken by the modern evolution of production [...] The outlook of the other classes (petty bourgeois or peasants) is ambiguous or sterile because their existence is not based exclusively on their role in the capitalist system of production (59).

As an exploitative class—and as profiteers of alienation—the bourgeoisie is thus aligned as an enemy of mankind itself. Given this view, the bourgeoisies—the villains of our story—take on an inhuman character: that of a creature and not a man; a monstrous and malignant enemy. Commenting upon the inhumanity of the rich, Rousseau emphasized that it was the bourgeois "state which steals from mine my children's bread" (qtd. in Beaud 57). The truth of the matter, however, is that our villain, like us, is not inhuman but *human*. And painfully so. We are her and she is us. So what, then, is the difference? By what ideological mechanism does a small subsection of humanity lord over the rest? And does such a mechanism have a material history? The haphazardness of present-day power relationships, it seems, is not enough to justify this imbalance. Other answers must be sought. And here we must turn to history: a history of that ideological force which is at the same time unreal yet imperative.

Where once the bourgeoisies were the burgher merchants, they are now the wealth-controlling business class—the suited inheritors of those feudal mercantilists—and their culture is that of blind accumulation: of business and of profit. Their holidays are the coopted feudal and indigenous holidays-turned-business; celebrated by a frenzy of spending. Their castles are the skyscrapers, and their social power rests upon the ownership of productive means, the accumulation of fiat currency, the control of exchange rates, and the revolutionizing of both production and product. Class analysis is not biological analysis, however. There are no organismic or biological markers which designate the bourgeoisie. To understand bourgeois ideology, however, along with bourgeois land relations, we must willingly accept a sort of murky reduction. A bicameral, two-classed view of society is both masterful yet reductive. It is masterful in that production-relations and the flow of wealth are properly conceptualized in an overarching two-tiered fashion; it is reductive in that the reality of the situation is much more complex. In between the two primary classes—the bourgeoisies (variegated into the upper, middle, and lower strata, or *haute, moyenne,* and *petite*) and the proletarians (also variegated into an administrative, skilled, and unskilled strata)—we have the shades of gray: the *lumpenproletariat,* the *precariat,* the remnants of feudal-era aristocracies, dukes and princes turned capitalists, religious monasticists, academicians, and so on. But, for simplicity's sake, and for the sake of the present argument—that is, to articulate the history of the capitalist problem as a *bourgeois* problem, and to seek the roots of now-global bourgeois land relations—we shall accept this seemingly simplistic reduction.

The capitalist "problem" is as follows. With the division of human society into hierarchies based upon a logic of profit, accumulation, and dominance, a vast, and underclass, majority of humanity has been thrust into a position of precariousness as *proletariat.* And proletarians must justify their existence through their labor in a world where the wealth produced by the economies of civil society—far more than enough to house and feed all—is withheld from them. This vast wealth lies forever beyond their reach; breadcrumbs alone are their fate. In 2017, in the U.S. alone, for example, there are approximately *six* empty houses for every *one* homeless person. The amount of wasted food, thrown out nightly and rotting from a lack of purchase, could feed scores of the starving. And medical treatment, daily, is withheld from those who cannot afford its luxury. The capitalist mode of production is problematic precisely because, *systemically,* its productive relations are structured in such a way as to withhold the bulk of the wealth of society from the masses of society itself. Why should we then agree to such a society? What is the point? The capitalist problem is a problem bound up within ideological and repressive state apparatuses, inequitable relations of production, and the ways in which the forces of production are owned by a dominant class to which all the benefits of capitalist society flows. Usage here of the analogy of the *pyramid scheme* would not be far from the truth.

The capitalist problem is not new, and yet it is also not ancient; it is, at most, around five hundred years in age. In 1616, for example, Antoine de Montchrétien, writing on the rise of French mercantilism, noted that, "The merchants are more than useful to the state, and their concern for profit which manifests itself in work and industry is what creates a good part of the public good" (qtd. in Beaud 36). Montchrétien captured the capitalist logic correctly when he also noted that, "We must have money, and if we have none from our own production, we must have some from foreigners" (qtd. in Beaud 37). Seen as a public good, blind to the damage it inflicts, bourgeois capitalism has been destructive precisely in that it has, historically, escaped its own psychoanalysis; it believes itself, unquestioningly, to be good. The logic of its repressed historical impetus remains hidden from its sight—either willingly or otherwise.

If we accept Kant's assertion, "[t]he means which nature employs to bring about the development of innate capacities is that of antagonism in society, in so far as this antagonism becomes in the long run the cause of a law-governed social order" (44), we might find ourselves tempted to accept this social antagonism as a force which is both good and beneficial in that a certain type of reckless homeostasis has been achieved via conflict and oppression; one which might be posited as an eternal solution—never to be questioned. But, if we take a critical, examined view of the *qualitative realness* of the world in which we live, we can easily see the inequities and the horrors of the present *produktionsweise*: mass incarcerations of subaltern populations, rampant exploitation, wars of both dominance and aggression, racism, poverty, alienation, and environmental destruction. For example, in 2017, *eight* multi-national individuals hold the same amount of material wealth as *fifty percent* of the globe's poorest population. This is not simply circumstantial; this financial disparity is built into the logic capitalism itself. It is a relationship of production which benefits one social class alone: the bourgeoisies. If we look hard enough, we might begin to question the current distribution of the wealth of civil society—dropping our assumptions that an exploitative mode of production is either good or beneficial to society at large. Indeed, we might see that the land itself is still held with a violence by those who wish to have more than others. Thus our bourgeoisie.

"One who has gold," noted Christopher Columbus in his 1492 travel log, "does as he wills in the world, and [...] even sends souls to paradise" (qtd. in Beaud 15). Following the flow of gold from the newly colonized and conquered areas of the world, the bourgeoisies, as merchants, found themselves enriched by the abundant spending of the kings and princes of Europe. Gold, which was taken both by conquest and by the murder of native populations, flowed from the coffers of the kings into the accounts of the merchants. Desiring opulence in the form of goods and crafts, the nobility spent lavishly, enriching, eventually, the merchants—our bourgeoisie—who thus became secondarily enriched by conquest; perhaps more so than the conquering nobility, if the arc of history is fully considered.

Historian Michel Beaud noted that "What Western history calls the 'great discoveries' enter at the junction of [a] twofold dynamic: in 1487 Bartholomeu Diáz rounded the Cape of Good Hope; in 1492 Christopher

Columbus discovered America; in 1498 Vasco de Gama, having skirted Africa, arrived in India. A great hunt after wealth—trade and pillage—began" (14). The end of the fifteenth century saw the beginning of a massive flooding of wealth into the kingdoms and cities of Europe; also, the material beginnings of the ennoblement and enrichment of the town-dwelling bourgeoisies—the beginning of the capitalist problem. Hernán Cortés captured the bourgeois impetus *in utero* when he confessed that, "We [...] suffer from a sickness of the heart for which gold is the only cure" (qtd. in Beaud 15). The bourgeois ethos of blind acquisition might have been born in the actions of the nobles, but it soon infected the minds of the merchants; the eventual torch of rulership passed down via the sickness of greed and dominance.

"According to official figures," wrote Beaud, "18,000 tons of silver and 200 tons of gold were transferred from America to Spain between 1521 and 1660; according to other estimates, double this amount" (15). Inversely proportional to the Spanish accumulation of gold were indigenous population numbers in the Americas: gold was acquired at the price of genocide. "In a little more than a century the Indian population was reduced by 90 percent in Mexico (where population fell from 25 million to 1.5 million), and by 95 percent in Peru" (Beaud 15). As American native populations declined, the wealth of the Spanish nobility, and the nobility of the concurrent European nobles who also took part in the plunder of the New World, rose sharply. And this wealth was spread widely—to the markets in Italy, France, Holland, and England (Beaud 15). The kings and queens spent, and the merchants profited. But with the flooding of precious metals into the feudal European economies, the signs of a new inflation became apparent. In Western Europe, the cost of wheat, whose price had remained relatively stable between 1500 and 1550, rose sharply—quadrupling between 1550 and 1600. In Spain:

> [P]rices tripled or quadrupled between the beginning of the sixteenth century and the beginning of the seventeenth century; in Italy the price of wheat rose by a factor of 3.3 between 1520 and 1599; between the first and the last quarter of the sixteenth century, prices rose by a factor of 2.6 in England and by 2.2 in France. In being diluted, the flow of precious metals reduced its effect on prices (Beaud 16).

During the sixteenth century, as the cost of goods rose, the real wages of those involved in early capitalist production decreased by fifty percent. As the ruling classes and mercantilists became increasingly wealthy, the poor suffered and were increasingly immiserated. "Popular discontent worsened and revolts of the poor broke out" (Beaud 16). Price controls were enacted, and confusion reigned as to the changing economy in Western Europe. A number of causes were investigated: "farmers, middlemen, exporters, foreigners, merchants, [...] usurers [and] 'monetary revaluations'" (16), but ultimately the cause of the discord was bound up within the obvious: a market flooded with a new abundance of currency in the form of precious metals: *inflation*, simply put.

J. Bodin, a jurist from Anjou, noted this at the time with an astute observation: "the principal and virtually sole cause of the rise in prices was the abundance of gold and silver which is greater today than it has been during the four previous centuries. [...] The principal cause of a rise in prices is always an abundance of that with which the prices of goods is measured" (qtd. in Beaud 16). However much this inflation hurt the poor in regards to the rising of costs and the decrease in real wages, the consensus was nonetheless held by the nobility and the mercantilist: "it is [ultimately] the abundance of precious metals which creates the wealth of the kingdom" (qtd. in Beaud 17).

In an effort to both stabilize and properly capitalize off of the new economic reality, laws were soon passed to prohibit gold from leaving national boundaries, and the ruling classes of the European nations focused on their own enrichment via an increase in the production of goods, and of manufacture: and for this, labor was of course needed. "The way was opened to the idea that the wealth of the kingdom depended on the wealth of the merchants and manufacturers" (Beaud 19). Following enclosure, an increase in land rents which changed the face of corvée labor, an emergent liberal philosophy embodied by such theorists as David Hume, and the flooding of European markets with wealth leading to an increase of goods and of production, the germ of capitalism slowly grew.

However, it was "[c]onquest, pillage, extermination: this [was] the reality out of which came the flow of precious metals to Europe in the sixteenth century" (Beaud 21). Michel Beaud noted that:

> Thus in the sixteenth century the conditions for the future development of capitalism were put into place: banking and merchant bourgeoisies having at their disposal both immense fortunes and banking and financial networks; national states having available the means for conquest and domination; and a conception of the world which valued wealth and enrichment. It

is this sense only that one can date the capitalist era as beginning in the sixteenth century (21).

Bourgeois dominance over the *ideological* glue of European society began to take shape during the sixteenth and seventeenth centuries. "Allied with the monarch because of their common interest in colonial expansion and mercantilism, the English bourgeoisie knew how to use popular discontent in its fight against absolutism, which was at the same time a fight for the strengthening of its own power" (Beaud 26). As the bourgeoisie class rose in social and material power, newly-enriched by the spending of the aristocracies, they soon turned their eyes towards political power—initially interested in achieving a political voice alongside the highest extant social class, the nobility. From 1610 to 1640, England's foreign trade alone increased tenfold, pushed along by a powerful productive machinery. Where earlier the ruling classes of the newly-enriched European nations had sought to hold on to their wealth, their accumulation of precious metals, a new logic began to emerge: one of international trade. Written in 1621, Thomas Mun's *Discourse on English Trade with the East Indies* "emphasized the importance of foreign trade: it was not so much a question of accumulating precious metals as of making them circulate in order to produce a positive balance" (qtd. in Beaud 27). Furthermore, in the 1662 *Report to the Private Council on Textiles*, a vision of bourgeoisie trade dominance was already being envisioned, evidenced by the following words of the report: "in each country a corporation should be established of those persons who are well-off and competent to control the proper fabrication" (qtd. in Beaud 27).

Early protectionism soon arose, and the bourgeoisies became entrenched as a power unto themselves: a growing consolidation of mercantile class power. From among the bourgeoisies, hand-in-hand with the great (capitalist) economic march forward, the philosophy of liberalism soon took hold. And philosophers rose to fulfill the challenge of crafting the theory of liberalism: David Hume, notably, who will be discussed at length in the following section.

Rousseau once noted that:

The first man who having enclosed a piece of land dared to say: "This is mine," and found people foolish enough to believe it, was the true founder of civil [bourgeois] society. How many crimes, wars and murders, how many miseries and horrors the human race would have been spared by the man who, tearing out the fence-stakes or filling in the ditch, shouted to his fellow creatures: 'Beware of listening to this imposter; you are lost if you forget that all the fruits of the earth are yours and that the earth itself is no one's!' (qtd. in Beaud 58).

Since Rousseau, not much has changed regarding the sentiments of those who do not own the land upon which they dwell. What has changed, however, is the degree to which the individual has become alienated from the land. The serf has slowly migrated to the city; the feudal subject has slowly become the capitalist subject—the proletarian. Michel Beaud wrote that, "Capitalism is neither a person nor an institution. It neither wills nor chooses. It is a logic at work through a mode of production: a blind, obstinate logic of accumulation" (129). Beaud went on to emphasize that:

> From the time that one speaks of capitalism as it has been historically realized, one must go beyond the single formula of a mode of production and its logic. There are nations in which capitalism has developed, and the rivalries between nations, though encouraged and characterized by the oppositions between national capitalisms, cannot be reduced to these oppositions. [...] There are ideas, beliefs, religions. The unstable duo of knowledge and ignorance, ideologies; there is racism, nationalism, militarism, the spirit of domination, and the spirit of profit (Beaud 130).

It is precisely this "spirit of profit" which we presently seek to deconstruct. This spirit of profit is woven throughout the ideology of the bourgeoisies, entailing a subsectional function: *bourgeois land relations*—the underlying environmental philosophy upon which capitalism itself is predicated.

To recapitulate our conception of the bourgeoisie: we hold that the dominant social class of the present capitalist epoch is one in which the wealth of society exists for—the poor, only to serve. Class analysis sits upon an historical analysis then, and the former may not exist without the latter. If we follow the opening proposition of the present work and resubmit that land—a portion of the earth to which a species owes its ability to both sustain and reproduce itself—is held, on the human social terrain, via violent force, then we can easily tease out the idea that violent force itself needs a locus of impact: an "other" against which violent force might posit itself. Thus enters our proletarian class; our alienated and exploited masses upon whom the yoke of oppression falls heaviest; against whom violence is directed.

The topographical-hierarchical class arrangement of society been long-critiqued by those on the bottom of such a topography. Rousseau himself, in a letter written in 1751, railed against this manner of social organization—the haves and the have-nots, the rich and the exploited poor, the bourgeoisie and the proletariat—when he wrote, tongue-in-cheek, "You [poor] need me, for I am rich and you are poor; let us then make an arrangement between ourselves; I will grant you the honor of serving me, on the condition that you give me the little you have left for the trouble I will take to order you about" (qtd. in Beaud 57). The capitalist problem is thus, at heart, a problem of class rule, of codified domination, and of so-called *civil* society's wealth being used for the betterment of a minute subsection of society itself. It is a problem of exploitation and of alienation: alienation of the poor masses from the very environment to which they owe their sustenance and reproduction, and the exploitation of surplus value from proletarian labor.

We submit that the problem of human alienation from the land itself, directed, as it is, upon the proletarian class, emerges from the economically-oriented hierarchical organization of class society. Economic-hierarchical social organization is nothing more than the control of land (entailing resources) in favor of one class at the expense of another. It is a violent land and resource-grabbing—an unfair allocation of the earth based upon a logic of both violence and dominance. Capitalism serves, ultimately, the bourgeoisies who do not represent, in numbers alone, the bulk of humanity. "The exploiting classes need political rule in order to maintain exploitation, i.e., in the selfish interests of an insignificant minority and against the interests of the vast majority of the people" (Lenin 287). Capitalist society thus poises itself as a species-destructive force; an absurd force—qua mode of production—which works against the better interests of the species which enacts its means, modes, and relations. But how can this be so? Let us consider a contrary position. The world presently exists in a state where there are now more humans than ever, where technological levels apparently provide never-before-seen comforts and entertainment, and where medical technology is such that we are able to extend the lives of those who might otherwise die. How can this be a bad thing? On the one hand, capitalism itself has generated an incredible amount of wealth for some parts of the human species; providing the species with an opportunity to flourish as never before, expanding populations to unheard of numbers—

into untouched regions of the globe. And, if we maintain the Kantian axiom that, "[a]ll the natural capacities of a creature are destined sooner or later to be developed completely and in conformity with their end" (Kant 42), might not our present era represent an era in which our natural capacities have been developed to their fullest? Are we at now our apex? Hardly.

Here we must remember that a temporary betterment of the living circumstances for a minute—what Lenin called an "insignificant" (287)—subsection of humanity does not in the least represent any sort of heaven-descended economic dictum, especially when that temporary inflation itself lies upon a resource-economy which views a *finite* set of resources as *infinite*. The capitalist mode of production thus entails, in its calculations, an ontological error. And as such, we have stumbled across yet another key—we might say *fundamental*—problematic of the capitalist *produktionsweise*: its unsustainable (and thus fallacious) economic foresight. The capitalist mode of production has bequeathed to us an increasingly tumultuous world in which a change of the globe's climate is most certainly caused, at least in part, by anthropogenesis. As the radix of capitalist economic praxis, bourgeois land relations—the structure of capitalist environmental philosophy—is a praxis-perspective which views the earth not as the qualitative sum of its parts, not as intrinsically valuable, and not as a life-supportive environment to be both maintained and preserved for posterity, but as a business venture: digital dismemberment for economic gain. Under the steadily-creeping dominance of this view, the earth is held as naught but a collection of values to be harvested for the profit of the bourgeoisies. This is the economic logic bequeathed to us by the early burgher merchants, by colonialism, and by imperialism.

Following all of this, bourgeois land relations might be held to be problematically absurd for this one glaring inanity: the utter unsustainability of the economic base they aver to legitimate predicates upon a myopia *orders of magnitude larger* than should be expected of such a self-interested social class. The class which benefits from the capitalist mode of production does not even have its own longevity in mind. How can the Marxists see this, but the capitalists cannot? What shall occur when the resources run dry? What shall occur when the last drop of oil has been combusted as fuel, and when the water of the earth has become polluted beyond salvation? The concept of infinite growth simply *cannot* work within an ontologically, and ecologically, finite system. When all of the oil has been pumped into the atmosphere as smoke, when our lungs burn from the inability to draw a breath, and when the land has been drained to the point of utter ruin, where then shall our species live? How will it both sustain and reproduce itself? How shall the capitalist then draw a profit?

The Ideological Radix of Bourgeois Land Relations

David Hume, in his *Enquiry Concerning Human Understanding*, once famously asserted, "Be a philosopher, but, amid all your philosophy, be still a man" (535). What, here, did Hume mean by the term "man"? What type of man would Hume have us be? The word "man" might at first carry with it connotations of gender identity, patriarchal masculinity, or sweeping historical stereotypes. The word alone does not offer us any answers which might be conceptualized outside of epochal or ideological contexts. Did Hume mean for us to act as the land-immersed, rural men of his day; or as the bourgeois men of business; or as the aristocratic men of leisure; or as the dispossessed proletarianized men—men forced into the early industrial landscape by the various enclosures? Here, Hume has no explicit answers for our question. However, upon a closer inspection of his work, the answer itself can indeed be teased out.

In his *Enquiry*, Hume defined man himself as being a reasonable, sociable, and active being (535)—stating that the world punished "abstruse thought and profound researches" with "severe melancholy" (535). In other words, and through a materialist lens, Hume maintained that the world rewarded reasoned social and economic action, but punished solitary introspection and disengagement from the marketplace. Surely, Hume's sentiment here cannot reflect a type of transcendental truism; rather, his statement must reflect at least an implicit epochal bias or at most a complicit and careful addition to the crafting of bourgeois ideology itself. Can Hume be seen a part of a larger philosophical movement to legitimate a capitalism of exploitation by way of a purposeful crafting of the social relationships of production—early liberalist theory? Can we paint the philosophical efforts of Hume with the brush of ideology itself?

On the surface, Hume's "be still a man" locution appears to be an exhortation against seclusionist, philosophical sophism. However, here we would suggest that Hume's statement might be indicative of the larger ideological movement of the capitalist epoch—one which worked to build the legitimating superstructure for the emerging, and rapidly industrializing, insidiousness of capitalism's productive mode—a mode founded on relationships of both exploitation and alienation. Hume's statement is a window into his perspectives—a peek into the mind of a man held to be an influential Western thinker—but it is also, in our opinion, a window into the history of bourgeois ideology, bound up as it is within the minds of ideologues such as David Hume and John Locke, Adam Smith, and others. Given the present-day earth-destructive trajectory of the capitalist productive mode, might we place some larger fault upon Hume's efforts? Was Hume himself to blame for contributing to the mass social acceptance of capitalism, of bourgeois class rule, or was his philosophy simply a product of the socio-economic trends of his era—a phenomenon stemming from "the ability in capitalism or any socio-economic system to create and control […] ethical beliefs" (Mehic 1). Held dialectically, and seen through the Marxist lens, the truth of course lies somewhere in the synthetic sublation of these two opposing positions.

Our assertion here is this: Hume indeed proposed a type of middle-capitalist sentiment—a stance which was patently pro-business, anti-religious, and unabashedly skeptical. Hume's ideas, interestingly, were those which stood in opposition to that which we might hold as the historical personage of the pre-capitalist philosopher: an individual withdrawn, contemplative, and world-critical—a philosopher like Diogenes, for example. Hume viewed these socially-margined philosophers to be philosophers of a lesser form, due to their incapability of "enter[ing] into business and action" (534). Here, Hume's privileging of social involvement and business, in contrast to the social un-involvement and rejected-mercantilism of the historical peripatetic/ascetic philosopher is telling of his views concerning the individual's relationship to the social arena, and to the marketplace. It seems here that, in Hume's view, the historically solitary philosopher had no market value. Teased out, we might then extend Hume's judgment upon humanity at large: serve the economy and do not be idle. Hume wrote that:

> The mere philosopher is a character which is commonly but little acceptable in the world, as being supposed to contribute nothing to either the advantage or the pleasure of society, while he lives remote from communication with mankind and is wrapped up in principles and notions equally remote from their comprehension. (534).

Hume, here, seems to imply that we should be of the entrepreneurial, capitalist type—a (wo)man with "an equal ability and taste for books, company, and business" (534). Emphasizing Hume's relationship to middle capitalism, Michel Beaud wrote that Hume indeed "stressed to the point of caricature the liberal logic according to which people have to be governed not by regulations and controls, but rather by their own interests" (75).

Hume himself wrote, in his *Independence of Parliament* (1741): "[The people's] greed must be made insatiable, their ambition beyond measure, and all their vices profitable for the public good" (qtd. in Beaud 75). Deconstructing Hume's usage of the term "public good" and inserting his definition for "man"—the intellectual, yet entrepreneurial, middle-capitalist—we begin to see hints that Hume's philosophical system might have been geared at helping and enriching but a select slice of the public: that of the profiteering capitalist—our dominating bourgeoisie class. And thus we can begin to envision Hume as a theorist for the bourgeoisies themselves: an apologist and a legitimator, hard at work to engender social support for an economic system that has society's interests least at heart.

Let us ask ourselves: Does the fostering of insatiable greed, ambition beyond measure, and profitable vices *truly* help the working public—those dispossessed and proletarianized ex-rurals, and the exploited and alienated masses who exist only to funnel the wealth of society upwards towards the topographical realm of the bourgeoisies? Did David Hume truly have the "public good" in mind? The answer, of course, is no. For the term "public good" Hume could only have meant the "good of the bourgeoisies."

If we accept the overtly bourgeois character of Hume's political theorizing, a question will soon present itself: to what extent do Hume's subtler philosophies—his ideas regarding metaphysics and ontology, presented in works such as his *Treatise, Dialogues,* and *Enquiry*—reinforce his pro-bourgeoisie mindset? To what extent do they legitimate capitalism itself and further the alienation of the individual from the land? Might we, for example, assert that Hume's refutation of the metaphysical subject—his gross reduction of the subject *into* the object and the subject relegated to naught but perceptions of the object; an anti-dialecticalism at heart—forms an almost skeletal metaphysical structure of bourgeois ideology, paving the way for capitalist entailments such as alienation and exploitation? Do Hume's ideas, in turn, lay the groundwork for bourgeois land relations and strengthen the endemic nature-alienation upon which it is founded? When Hume states that, "I may venture to affirm of the rest of mankind that they are nothing but a bundle of perceptions which succeed each other with an inconceivable rapidity" (526), does he do this in purposeful support of the historical trajectory of the bourgeoisies, of whom he was a part? Did Hume intend upon depriving the proletarianized masses of their very souls?

We might also ask ourselves if these types of philosophical assertions, in some way, deprive the masses of their last psychological protection against capitalist productive relations. Would the "vulgar superstitions" (636), against which Hume argued so consistently—manifested in the positions of phenomenologically-oriented philosophers such as George Berkeley—actually serve to weaken bourgeois class rule, and might this one of the reasons for Hume's subtle rebuttals to Berkeley (561)? Does Hume's mitigated skepticism in regards to matters of god, self, and universe, actually pave the way for the increasing consumerization of society; for the proletarianization of the poor; and for the ideological insulation of the bourgeoisies themselves?

Whether or not David Hume actually intended to spread the economic discourse of capitalism through his philosophy, and whether or not he knew of the long term and far reaching implications of his work is of course unknown to us. Through the lens of Hume, it seems that all that we are able to know is our "profound ignorance" (562). How fortunate. Hume himself refutes any certitude in that "[t]he relation of cause and effect must be utterly unknown to mankind" (565).

Let us move on to some structural support for our ideas, with only a minor recapitulation of our previous section, enumerated in the following points.

1. Moving out of the vestiges of the epoch of three-estate feudalism (Beaud 13), capitalism emerged, historically, as a *new* socio-economic order—a new mode of production—eventually privileging the "merchant and monetary societies" (Beaud 11) over the hereditary nobility.
2. Human society is comprised of both material and ideological components.
3. The rise of the bourgeoisie predicated, then, upon both material and ideological revolutions in European feudal culture.
4. Beginning in earnest with the influx of gold from the Americas during the fifteenth and sixteenth centuries (Beaud 15), and as wealth soon funneled into the hands of the mercantilists, a power shift began to occur: power moved away from the nobility and into the hands of the emergent bourgeoisie class (Beaud 21).
5. But, for a true transfer of power to occur—for the emergence of a new social order, one dominated by the bourgeoisie and not the traditional nobility—and for the legitimation of a new class of

aristocracy, ideological transformation had to occur. For the poor to accept the rule of yet another class, a system of legitimation needed to be in place.

6. For this to happen, traditional power structures had to be dissolved, and public opinion had to be swayed into the overthrow of the old ruling class and towards the acceptance of a new ruling class. Ideological transformation, in the form of a revolutionizing of ideology, was needed.

7. Partly by way of the concerted efforts of bourgeois philosophers, partly by way of the material forces of history, theoreticians and ideologues began to lay the groundwork for the new ruling class through, for example:
    a. Hume's de-legitimation of the spiritual sovereign, the Catholic church;
    b. Locke's de-legitimation of the political sovereign, the king;
    c. and Hume's de-legitimation of the individual sovereign— of antithetical ideological perspectives, such as George Berkeley's phenomenological, immaterialist philosophy which places the individual at the center of his or her own reality.

8. The exemplifier of this philosophy of de-legitimation through a position of absolute uncertainty and (patently mitigated) skepticism was David Hume.

9. Hume's ontology, with its proclamation of theistic un-knowability, noncommittal compatabilism, and unmitigated skepticism helped to erase, both psychologically and ideologically, the mental stumbling blocks which lie in the way of a full public acceptance of capitalism and with it, bourgeois class rule.

10. Hume's association of religion with terror (639) and his relegation of the substance of mental self to naught but a series of perceptions (526) seeks, in our view, to *philosophically* dispossess the masses by extricating them from their cultural and religious philosophies, thus fulfilling 2 and 4, and paving the way for the eventual fulfillment of 1.

Again, while we cannot know for certain whether Hume intended his theorizing—and more specifically his ontology—to feed into the growing legitimation of bourgeois capitalism, it does, following points 1 through

8, at least appear that way. Here it would also be good to remember that Hume was good friends with the early capitalist theorist Adam Smith.

Our purpose in producing the previous chain of reasoning has primarily been in response to the words of Hume himself: "[b]ut if you insist that the inference is made by a chain of reasoning, I desire you to produce that reasoning" (546). We have hopefully made no great jumps in logic—our failings, potentially, lying only in a lack of a full explanation of points 7 and 8. These failings might beg the question: from where did we infer that skepticism and an uncertain ontology necessarily leads to an acceptance of capitalist (qua bourgeois) economic ideology? Let us attempt an answer.

Using the Marxist theoretical conception of the tensioned dialectical relationship between economic/material base and ideological/cultural superstructure, we began to reason, simply in fact, that the underlying economic system of Hume's time—the base—of middle stage capitalism *had* to have some formative impact on Hume's philosophy, which naturally occupied the domain of the superstructure of eighteenth century English culture. And, as a dialectic, we also reasoned that Hume's philosophy began to legitimate the existing economic base—which then, again, further entrenched the superstructure in new and insidious ways. Herein lies the essential statement of the dialectic: to paraphrase a young Karl Marx, the two discrete forces (economic and ideological) are distinct, yet form a unity ("Early Writings" 158). Assuming the dialectical sublation of both base and superstructure, or, at the very least, a one-way informative relationship from base *to* superstructure, it seemed only natural that the skepticism and uncertain ontology developed by Hume would *naturally* seek to further entrench the base—however oppressive and immoral it may have presented itself. Here, we might also wonder if the rejection, or, worse, the *cooption*, of autonomous reason leaves us with only our passions and desires in the marketplace?

By robbing his readers of any ontological or metaphysical certitude, we can begin to see how Hume might have opened the door for the rising power structure—the bourgeoisie class—to prey upon that public uncertainty, thereby allowing the bourgeoisies to create their own illusions of certainty. As the masses were led to question ideas of sovereignty under the guise of "the public good," the bourgeoisie might have used this opportunity to foment revolutions, overthrow the historical power structures of both monarch and church, co-opt the poor into their cause, and create power vacuums, thus utilizing the chaos of the emergence of the new world order to assert their dominance.

The Cooption of Reason: Subverting the Proletarian Mind

On the faculty of human reason, Max Horkheimer, in his essay entitled *The End of Reason*, wrote that, "Its features can be summarized as the optimum adaptation of means to ends, thinking as an energy-conserving operation. It is a pragmatic instrument oriented to expediency, cold and sober" (28). According to Horkheimer, the pragmatic nature of reason is itself prosaic; an example of human psychology adapting itself to its material circumstances—weighing options, and charting a most efficient course. But reason itself, Horkheimer continued, is subject to both social and political trends. Our previous example of David Hume bears witness to this. By way of humanism, reason as an energy-conserving device turns its lens upon what is best for both the individual *and* society. And in this way, its individualistic nature is easily subverted: turned outwards, reason becomes a normalizing force, a force with which to subvert the will of the individual towards the will of the collective. This is important given that the collective typically enforces a codified rule by hierarchy. In its basest of forms, social-reason becomes patriotism. Horkheimer quotes De Maistre, who claims that patriotism is, "that national reason […]; it is the abnegation of the individual" (29). Reason, once extrapolated out towards the so-called "public good" of Hume, and once it has fallen sway to the impulses—overt or otherwise—of the dominant class of a collective, negates the individual; it can negate his best interest. In collective reasoning, one can reason against his better interests, thus negating the purpose of reason itself.

It is this exploitation of the considerational faculty of humanity, a faculty which "from the very beginning included the concept of critique" (Horkheimer 27), that Marcuse addresses when he wrote that, "[f]ascism and militarism have developed a deadly efficient solidarity" (88). Or, in other words, militaristic (bourgeois) fascism has coopted social-reason to such a degree as to mobilize its subjects—willing or otherwise—into a powerful and dominating force. Marcuse went on to suggest that the individualist reclamation of reason, the reclamation of critique itself, was indeed a modus operandi of the socialist project, that great push-back against capitalism and bourgeois class rule: "Socialist solidarity is autonomy: self-determination begins at home—and that is with every I, and the We whom the I chooses" (88). Or, in other words, reason, once freed, becomes liberatory; "[i]f it could lead to self-determination at the very base of human existence, it would be the most radical and most complete revolution in human history" (45).

28

Having thus been subverted by the bourgeois *élites* of the now-global polis—those rulers and beneficiaries of forced hierarchy and oppressive stratification—reason has since fallen sway to bourgeois ideology itself. Considering Hume's bourgeois-locus "public good"—that good which, in the US, is presently decided by the corporate *élite* and ruling class interest; that militaristic and fascist solidarity—discourse is thus shaped and reason is coopted. Following the example of the recent 2016 U.S. presidential election, a small selection of choices (two, in fact) are presented to the individual thinking subject, and the coopted reason is left only to select that choice which is presented as most efficient, expedient, and energy-conserving. This seems to indicate what Horkheimer called "the self-preserving rationality of the *élites*" (47). By way of shaping discourse, shaping reason, the "dictatorship" of the bourgeoisie continues unfettered by popular resistance.

Even the alleged resistance to the present capitalist trajectory, that resistance which supposedly takes form as capitalist revisionism, in Democratic Party activism (which has *always* sought to enforce the capitalist status quo), in Social Democratic reform, and so on, has already been coopted and serves the political trajectory of the present dictatorship itself. Revolution is thus presented to the thinking subject only as a reproductive tool of capitalism itself. Far from being opposed to the capitalist system, it is but a part of its self-preserving rationality. As the caricatured monstrosity of Donald Trump has ascended the throne of U.S.-locus capitalist administration, the *élites* get what they have wanted all along: a continued dictatorship where bourgeois administrators are decided, not elected. And this decision takes shape via the manufactured consent of the individual: a consent which presents itself as an exercising of reason; but a consent which has been altogether manufactured by the patriotic rationality of "the public good."

The individual's reason—that faculty which separates him from the other animals of the world (Horkheimer 26)—is bought and sold back to him without his recognition of the sale. Regarding political discourse alone, the individual reasons to himself that the lesser of evils is the better of choices, the most expedient; he is unaware—or ideologically ignorant—that there are options available to him in which evil is *not* present. There are socialist alternatives. The individual reasons alone in a world after the image of the bourgeoisie: a world which the bourgeoisie has crafted, in which all choices represent an evil. This world, the narrative of which has been presented to us from birth as a matrix of bourgeois ideology, which itself entails bourgeois land relationships, is the world in which co-opted reason presents itself to us as pure reason. The world of the bourgeoisie is thus a false world, predicated upon what Friedrich Engels called *false consciousness*. Inside of a false world, a false consciousness may only exercise false reason. Here, in all senses, "false" is analogous to "coopted."

Horkheimer wrote that, "Reason has borne a true relation not only to one's own existence but to living as such; this function of transcending self-preservation is concomitant with self-preservation, with obeying and adapting to objective ends" (47). Reason falls sway, then, to both discourse *and* biology. "[T]he ideological incorporation of men into society takes place through their 'biological' pre-formation for the controlled collectivity" (Horkheimer 47). A fairly simplistic syllogism can thus be constructed to offer some structural support for our logic:

1. As both a social animal and a species-being, man's own individual self-interest *becomes* the self-interest of the collective.
2. The self-interest of the collective is shaped by the will of the ruing *élites*.
3. Man's own *self*-interest is thus shaped by the will of the ruling *élites*.

Reason, then, is both man's blessing and curse: it is his individual capacity to chart a most expedient course through the social and material terrain of life. And it is also the vehicle through which he is most easily led astray—towards his own volunteered enslavement as an economic subject of the capitalist system; a subject of the bourgeoisie class. When extrapolated out towards a most expedient route for the collective, massy reason quickly falls sway to the decisions of but a few.

In *One-Dimensional Man*, Marcuse wrote that, "Those whose life is the hell of the Affluent Society are kept in line by a brutality which revives medieval and early modern practices" (23). While Marcuse is indeed correct in his claim, it seems that, following our line of reasoning, an even more insidious brutality is enacted by way of the cooption of reason. Proletarian class consciousness is, in this way, kept muddled and distant by bourgeois manufacture. The proletariat takes bourgeois class interest to be her own and unwittingly—by way of her reason—reasons the bourgeois socioeconomic interests to be in her own *best* interest. Lukács wrote that, "For a class to be ripe for hegemony means that its interests and consciousness enable it to organize the whole of society in accordance with those interests" (52). The whole of American society is indeed mobilized towards a singular, albeit false, objective: the continued dominance of the bourgeoisie class and the continued dominance of capitalist economy. This false organization of society takes clear shape in the manufacturing of consent by way of the bourgeois cooption of proletarian reason. Popular opinion is thus relegated only to a manufactured consent by way of both a discursive and ideological cooption of the individual's faculty to discern the most expedient and efficient course for both self and society. This false (coopted) organization, far from trope is, in essence, fascistic. "Fascism characterizes the stage at which the individual has completely lost his independence and the ruling groups have become recognized by the state as the sole legal parties to political compromise" (Kirchheimer 70). Bourgeois class rule is thus a type of fascism.

All of the aforementioned seems to point quite obviously to what Marcuse called the *one-dimensional* society. "By virtue of the way it has organized its technological base, contemporary industrial society tends to be totalitarian. For 'totalitarian' is not only a terroristic political coordination of society, but also a non-terroristic economic-technical coordination which operates through the manipulation of needs by vested interests" (3). What Marcuse seems to be saying here is this: further than the bourgeois cooption of the proletarian's individual reason, what is more strongly at play within unidimensional bourgeois social structure is a cooption of individual and mass technological need. "Independence of thought, autonomy, and the right to political opposition are being deprived of their basic critical function in a society which seems increasingly capable of satisfying the needs of the individuals through the way in which it is organized" ("One-Dimensional Man" 1). Here, bourgeois control of society, and of land, seems total: both the technical/economic base and cultural/reasoning superstructure are accounted for. The individual's thinking and reasoning mind is controlled, but allowed to think itself free; the individual's position, his wants, production, and consumption are also tightly controlled—further, they are manufactured.

In the modern, post-Soviet era, with no visible, large-scale opposition to the capitalist mode of production, bourgeois dominance over global society *is* total. Not only is society itself one-dimensional, but the world as well. In 1969, Marcuse wrote that, "The growing opposition to the global dominion of corporate capitalism is confronted by the sustained power of this dominion: its economic and military hold in the four continents, its neocolonial empire, and, most important, its unshaken capacity to subject the majority of the underlying population to its productivity and force" (vii). Today the situation seems much more grim.

Otto Kirchheimer commented on the historical rise of one-dimensional society by stating that, "The automatic integration of the political structure by money in the nineteenth century and the systematic use of the credit apparatus to this end in the period of mass democracy has given way to forms of domination by institutionalized monopolies" (58). While he continued by saying that, "[t]hese changes have occurred in their most pointed form in Germany" (58), once could (by way of his reference to the political dominance of institutionalized monopolies) easily tease out the conclusion that the U.S. is currently *the* fascist state par excellence towards which the new critique must be focused. The joinder of state and corporate institutions—the sharing of political power by businesses and administrators as a unique function of the fascist society— seems further emphasized by Kirchheimer, who wrote that "every increase in organizational power granted to the private industrial and trade associations is accompanied by an increase in the supervisory power of the corresponding government agencies" (59). Even if the governmental regulatory bodies exists as paper tigers only, the growth of both forces together—business and government—and their creeping dominion over the globe, can only indicate a fascistic trend. In Kirchheimer's *Changes in the Structure of Political Compromise* one can see reflections of the American moment: "The slow disappearance of the small businessman is speeding up; shops are closed if they are deemed unnecessary for the national economy, the debts, as far as is thought advisable, are paid off by official organizations, and the former shopkeepers are sent off to the factory" (61).

The insidiousness of the domination of bourgeois ideology is that while all the signs of fascism are present, it is not the strong-armed governmental organizations sending the small shopkeeper to the factories; rather, the small shopkeeper closes her own doors due to the ideological and material hegemony of the large companies, folding herself to the supposedly "free" market pressures which are, in actuality, not free at all, but heavily regulated. This is how ideology works: we think ourselves to be free, yet we imprison ourselves—unable to even articulate our own unfreedom for lack of an ideological structure in which to do so. The small shopkeeper, following the cooption of both her reason and economic interest by bourgeois class interests, self-polices; she sends herself to the factory. The domination of bourgeois ideology legitimates her choice by having her feel that what has happened is both natural and inevitable; a result of her reason as she selects a most efficient course given her circumstances. She then wanders off to the voting booth, only to then to perpetuate her situation by way of a false democracy. Her reason coopted, she is persuaded to select against her own class interest.

"[D]emocracy does not exist," Marcuse wrote, "and the government is factually exercised by a network of pressure groups and 'machines,' vested interests represented by and working on and through the democratic institutions" ("One-Dimensional Man" 70). The insidiousness of the whole system lies in its absolute invisibility to its subjects; yet it is the elephant in the room. The proletarian individual—the collection of which far outnumber the bourgeois *élites*—compromises her freedom for economic slavery, an example of both the "dehumanized and dehumanizing function of the commodity relation" (Lukács 92), the coopted reason which would have her believe that the capitalist world is natural and inevitable: a one-dimensional totality. The result is a sort of glamour enacted upon the proletarian public by the bourgeois *élites*; more creeping and devious than direct domination under the iron glove—the self-capitulation to bourgeois class rule is a self-enslavement.

The Machine of Civil Society

Hannah Arendt once wrote, in her classic text *Eichmann in Jerusalem: A Report on the Banality of Evil*, that, "The trouble with Eichmann was precisely that so many were like him, and that many were neither perverted nor sadistic, that they were, and still are, terrifyingly normal" (276). The same could be said of the hegemony of bourgeois class rule, held in sway, furthered, and reproduced, as it is, by bourgeois ideology: that it is precisely within its terrifying mundanity and normality that it has become so pervasive, so total, and so troubling. In our view, bourgeois ideology, having a now-total global reach, has become so insurmountable, and so ubiquitous, *precisely* because of its banality. It is not the overt fascism of Mussolini, but rather the "friendly fascism" of Bertram Gross's analysis; it conceals its ugliness beneath a façade of inclusiveness, of liberalism, and thus it masks its truth behind falsity. Earth-destructive capitalism, by way of its cultural superstructure, masquerades itself as benevolent through such (false) concepts as democracy, radical individualism, and purported social betterments, but it is within these masquerades specifically—these false presentations—that its insidiousness is revealed. It presents itself as unarguable: a result of the inevitability of human progress, but it is, however, one system amidst a history of systems. Its ideologues have worked hard to present such a system as unarguable. Actual resistance—its overthrow—is, as of yet, unrealized; its ideological and material cooption of all heretofore oppositional systems has yet to leave a viable subversive force which has been able to escape nor surmount its grasp.

The banality of bourgeois ideology enacts itself through both the mundane and the (de)sublime: it pervades art, public discourse, media, and education. And its growth appears proportionate to the growth of technology. As technology advances, ever on its heels is the legitimative force of ideology—reacting back upon its base to further the growth and adoption of technology in ways that reinforce and drive ideology itself.

Walter Benjamin theorized the degradation of art by way of technology when he wrote that, "I can no longer think what I want to think. My thoughts have been replaced by moving images" (42). Here Benjamin critiqued the film—the moving picture. He exclaimed to us that in the age prior to the mechanical reproduction of art, one might stand before a painting for hours, losing oneself into the presentation of the image—our thoughts sublimating towards speculation and rumination. The painting existed as a device by which we might engage in abstraction, following our thoughts and adding new hues to our reason. "A man who concentrates before a work of art is absorbed by it" (43), Benjamin wrote. But, for Benjamin, after the onset of the age of mechanical reproduction, art no longer engaged the individual; rather, the individual devoured the art, yet only in passivity. The individual sitting in front of the movie screen became a passive recipient of the agenda of the filmmaker; no thought required. Now, Benjamin wrote, "the distracted mass absorbs the work of art" (43). Art, like reason, has thus been coopted and politicized as an ideology-imparting device.

As Theodor Adorno noted in his essay *Freudian Theory and the Pattern of Fascist Propaganda*, "The so-called psychology of fascism is largely engendered by manipulation. Rationally calculated techniques bring about what is naively regarded as the 'natural' irrationality of the masses" (135). Here, one is reminded of the American bourgeois war-film industry. Where is the film which portrays the horrors of expansionist wars of aggression outside of absorptive spectaclization? Films like "American Sniper," amidst a mass of others, serve only to facilitate the war machine; to reinforce the idealism of a war-focused American public. And further, such films emphasize the cult of the individual; not only are they idealistic, they are also profoundly ideological in nature. They portray so-called heroes as the driving forces of history, when in actuality it has always ever been the masses who move history forward. Such films implant ideas by way of direct manipulation—what Benjamin called the "spell of

34

personality" (31), and which he went on to call that "phony spell of the commodity" (31). Adorno poignantly noted that:

> It may well be that the secret of fascist propaganda that it simply takes men for what they are: true children of today's standardized mass culture, largely robbed of autonomy and spontaneity, instead of setting goals the realization of which would transcend the psychological *status quo* no less than the social one. Fascist propaganda has only to *reproduce* the existent mentality for its own purposes;—it need not induce a change—and the compulsive repetition which is one of its foremost characteristics will be at one with the necessity for this continuous reproduction (134).

The psychological structure of (friendly) fascist culture is already entrenched; its reproducers and contrivers only need to perpetuate what is already there; exploit what is already warped.

The true insidiousness of bourgeois ideology is that those most hurt by its existence are amongst its largest and most fervent supporters: as art, media, public discourse, and political theory, bourgeois ideology— entailing our bourgeois land relations—is reproduced *ad nauseum* by the public in general. And not that the true enslaving, oppressive qualities of ideology originate within the public social base—the discourse, on certain levels, has been shaped and prodded by those in the know—but that the public is, by and large, blindly obedient to what they are presented with: a ready-made culture to which their only duty is bound up within reproduction and perpetuation. Obedience to the superstructural status quo is both assumed and the line is toed; but, as Hannah Arendt noted, "politics is not like the nursery; in politics obedience and support are the same" (279). An obedience to, and a furtherance of, bourgeois ideology is a support of its oppression, its resultant destruction, and its war-horrors. Walter Benjamin's moving picture has become the scrolling screen of the iPhone and the mini-worlds of "social" media: Facebook, Instagram, Twitter, and so on. We are still passive receivers of the pictures, politicized sloganizing, memes, and mundanities which scroll past our eyes, and with every like and up-vote, we seem to be guilty of both obedience and support, adding in our own two-cents as long as it fits within the ideological status quo.

Benjamin noted that:

> Fascism attempts to organize the newly created proletarian masses without affecting the property structure which the masses strive to eliminate. Fascism sees its salvation in giving these masses not their right, but instead a chance to express themselves. The masses have a right to change property relations; Fascism seeks to give them an expression while preserving property. The logical result of Fascism is the introduction of aesthetics into political life (47).

Regarding nature, and the land relations proffered by bourgeois ideology, the pervasiveness of earth-saving, liberal documentaries such as the recent "Jumbo Wild" seem to hint at an underbelly of discontent; an albeit coopted recognition of capitalism's destruction of the earth. Documentaries exposing the discontent with the hyper-monetized medical industry, the hyper-monetized food industry, etc., seem to hint at what Benjamin called "the property structure which the masses strive to eliminate" (47). Every upset is, ultimately, an upset with bourgeois capitalism. However, the ubiquity of bourgeois ideology, the strength of bourgeois hegemony, and the ignorance to both critical and Marxist class analysis never moves the discontent towards political action; it never moves beyond a grumbling. At most, useless petitions are filed via change.org. True change never seems to come about. The liberal masses thus go on reproducing bourgeois ideology ad infinitum; acting as the architects of their own futility. This seems reminiscent, on some level, of what Adorno called, "the Nazi slogan that 'only sacrifice makes us free'" (306). In this case the sacrifice is oneself; the freedom naught but enslavement to an economic order which benefits those few *élites*.

There is a quality which seems to be inculcated by bourgeois ideology, and upon which Benjamin writes, of passive receptivity in regards to the individual's relationship towards his native cultural machine. This passive receptivity seems analogous to what Adorno called *regressive listening*. "Regressive listening," he wrote, "is tied to production by the machinery of distribution, and particularly by advertising." He went on to say that:

> Regressive listening appears as soon as advertising turns into terror, as soon as nothing is left for the consciousness but to capitulate before the superior power of the advertised stuff and

purchase spiritual peace by making the imposed goods literally its own thing (287).

This quality of regressive listening, of passive receptivity, seems to have its genesis within the advertising structure—that selling-vehicle which works by creating a lack, a need, in the individual, and then selling to that void. Under the hegemonic dominance of both the capitalist mode of production and the advertising model, an entire global civilization of empty subjects—subjects who are constantly propagandized by way of advertising into believing that they are incomplete beings and must seek their completeness via material gain—seem to have fallen sway to an alienating inversion of the subject-object relationship whereby the man, as prior subject, becomes an object to the new subject of his goods.

"Man is a result," Adorno wrote, "not an *eidos*" (511), and as a result, his participation and complicity with bourgeois society and economy seem to be but a result of the trajectory of the species, working, as it does (and if Kant is correct) towards a "universal civic society" (Kant 4); its purpose bound up within the overall "public good." However, in the present case, the good of the public, of the species, has deferred to the good of the public's *élite* ruling class; or maybe it has always been this way. The terrifying normality of it all, along with the problematic ubiquity of public complicity, work together to create a quagmire from which the chances of escape seem slim. Ideology is shown to the public, and "[t]he public is an examiner, but an absent-minded one" (Benjamin 45). "This," wrote Benjamin, "is the situation of politics which Fascism is rendering aesthetic" (49).

Weaponized Curriculum

It serves us now to examine one of the most powerful ways in which bourgeois ideology is reproduced inside of civil society. In our analysis, this takes shape primarily by way of public education—that appendage which exists on the cusp of the ideological and the repressive, in which young minds are held captive from the ages of five (if not younger) to eighteen; our ideological formation taking shape along bourgeois state lines; thirteen years (give or take) of state-mandated, and direct, indoctrination.

In his classic text on education, *Pedagogy of the Oppressed*, Paulo Freire wrote that a "careful analysis of the teacher-student relationship at any level, inside or outside the school, reveals its fundamentally narrative character. This relationship involves a narrating Subject (the teacher) and patient, listening Objects (the students)" (71). Entailed within every narrative are the ideological qualities which are imparted—knowingly or unknowingly—as well as both content and, in the case of education, grade-specific curricula. Ideology here takes the shape of the dominant cultural discourse; that Gramscian *cultural hegemony* of bourgeois class rule which sees the purposive warping of innate and naturally emerging tendencies towards both shaped and sculpted discourse—the repetition of a cultural fabric which props up an *élite* class by way of legitimation, and subjugates the majority to those *élites'* wills.

A pedagogy of the oppressed—an attempt by the majority to reclaim the narrative, to reclaim their education in their own best interests—is one which sets itself in opposition to the *taught* cultural hegemony; in opposition to *taught* bourgeois ideology. The existence of a radical pedagogy, a critical pedagogy, or a communist pedagogy, presupposes a dominant opposition; its very presence, as well as its methodology, paints a clear picture, in negative, of the subtle dogma against which it teaches.

In this section, our efforts will be directed towards both the discussion and elaboration of the following ideas:

1. Radical education—specifically the critical pedagogical stance—sets itself up in antithetical opposition to the thetic, dominant form of bourgeois education. Radical education exists to combat a bourgeois ideology which is taught.

2. *Taught* bourgeois ideology—what in *Teaching to Transgress* bell hooks called the "banking system of education" (40)—is nothing but the material, intentional reproduction of the bourgeois cultural hegemony via an aspect of the ideological state apparatus. It is not an abstract force; it is not mystical. Rather, it is directly taught, reproduced and entrenched via public, state curricula and bourgeois pedagogy.

3. Radical education occupies a pedagogical stance which teaches, directly, modes and ways of being and thinking which run contrary to the modes and ways of being of bourgeois ideology—where bourgeois education alienates, radical education seeks to unalienate, and where bourgeois education proletarianizes populations based upon their economic geography, radical education seeks to unproletarianize, working to free its students from both economic and ideological bondage. In this regard, radical education via a critical pedagogy can be seen as a liberatory education—one which seeks to free humans from the economic

yoke of bourgeois capitalism, and one which seeks to move humanity towards a stage of higher global communism—that classless, stateless, free, and creative international community of individuals upon which Marx and Engels theorized and predicted to emerge, post-capitalism and post-socialism.

Georg Lukács wrote that, "[T]he bourgeoisie has the intellectual, organizational and every other advantage, the superiority of the proletariat must lie exclusively in its ability to see society from the centre, as a coherent whole" (69). It is precisely this coherent wholism of which Paulo Freire spoke when he mentioned that his educational project—his *pedagogy of the oppressed*—"must come, however, from the oppressed themselves and from those who are truly solidary with them" (45). What these statements seem to hint at are what we see as several key entailments of the bourgeois educational model: (a) that bourgeois educational dominance is endemic to capitalist class society—its mode of education reproduces its own manner of class rule, inculcates economic subservience, and indoctrinates the revolving young of capitalist society to accept radically counterintuitive conceptual frameworks of bourgeois democracy, capitalist economics, and *élite* class rule; and (b) that any progressive education which sets itself in opposition to bourgeois class society must, in addition to being in opposition to the pervasive oppressor ideology, emerge from those downtrodden of the society itself. As labor organizer Lucy Parsons once wrote, "Never be deceived that the rich will allow you to vote away their wealth"; neither will the rich allow the ideological legitimation of their rule to be taught away by a public, state-enforced curricula.

Paulo Freire emphasized that, "the pedagogy of the oppressed cannot be developed or practiced by the oppressors. It would be a contradiction in terms if the oppressors not only defended but actually implemented a liberating education" (54). In praxis, this has definite and clear implications—the oppressed must liberate themselves; their liberation will not be granted by their oppressors. Via an examination into oppositional educational models, some insight is shed, in negative, upon the machinations and totalizing methodology of bourgeois ideological dominance, which in turn sheds some light upon both its character and its methods of reproduction. It paints a picture of the thing against which the entire communist project at large is aligned, and sheds interesting and new light on its social aspects. By examining the ways in which educators such as Freire and hooks teach against the status quo, we may begin to see traces of the ways in which the status quo itself is taught: its emphasis on opening ever-new markets, its desire for the perpetual creation of ever-new workforces, its goals in corralling the thoughts of its subjects, and its emphasis on presenting itself as the only option—a force against which nothing might be counterposed.

As a mentally oppressive force, legitimating itself and planting the seeds of its own reproduction into the minds of its subjects, bourgeois ideology exists, primarily, within the immaterial world of ideas—it can be thought of, on one hand, as an abstract force. It exists in ideas and intentions, and does not consist of any material shape; only its psychological effects are felt. The theoretical-terminological device *bourgeois ideology*, even, is an equally abstract term upon an already abstract conception. Upon examination, and via the Wittgensteinian lens (we will discuss Wittgenstein further in the next chapter), the term almost dissolves into meaninglessness. But, on the other hand, bourgeois ideology can be traced to some very material, and very concrete, things: notwithstanding its material support for the economic base of capitalism, bourgeois ideology is *taught by way of public school curriculum*. Its character and content may be examined, materially, in the lesson books—the vector of delivery—of the various state and public school curricula. And it is delivered by way of pedagogy: a pedagogy which we can call, with a nod to Freire, a pedagogy of the oppressor. Bourgeois ideology's unique (false) narrative of history can be thoroughly examined by way of an examination of its textbooks; its preferences might be determined by way of its standardized tests; and its intents might be gleaned by way of its pedagogical delivery: its eight-hour school day with two fifteen-minute breaks and a half hour lunch, its training towards the clock and the bell, and its obedience-heavy character all belie its underlying proletarianizing intentions. The pedagogy of the oppressor seeks, ultimately, to train workers. It seeks to break spirits and to ingrain radically counterintuitive ideas: that one must surrender oneself to work, that work is the only recourse, and that if one but works hard enough, one might actually escape the prison of coerced labor. In other words, the pedagogy of the oppressor aims to ingrain into our minds that *arbeit macht frei*.

This dual-view that the culturally hegemonic ideology itself is both an abstract ideological force *and* has definite material components by way of its pedagogy and curriculum is most correctly conceptualized dialectically: the truth lies somewhere in the combination, negation, and sublation of the material and ideological factors. Both abstract ideas and concrete *materia* work together to create new and evolving forms which become ever new and dominating frameworks by which humanity is subjugated to the economic will of bourgeois *élites*. However, within these sublations lie some very real and concrete ways by which the capitalist project may be subverted. If pedagogy and curricula are ways through which the capitalist socio-economic agenda perpetuates itself, then oppositional pedagogies—those aimed at dismantling the "myths created and developed in the old order, [those] which like spectres haunt the new structures emerging from the revolutionary transformation" (Freire 55)—exist as praxis for the revolution itself. Bourgeois ideology, bourgeois land relations, and the earth-destructive, material force of capitalism have the potential to be subverted, in part, via *educational* means. And this is a comforting thought.

Marx and Engels, in *The German Ideology*, wrote that:

> In direct contrast to German philosophy which descends from heaven to earth, here we ascend from earth to heaven. That is to say, we do not set out from what men say, imagine, or conceive, nor from men as narrated, thought of, imagined, conceived, in order to arrive at man in the flesh. We set out from real, active men, and on the basis of their real life-process we demonstrate the development of the ideological reflexes and echoes of this life-process. (14)

What Marx and Engels pointed to, here, was a foundational theoretical piece upon which, in our view, the entire communist project lay, critical pedagogy notwithstanding: that there is a way to view human social relations which is, itself, both dialectical and scientific—that Kantian way of conceptualizing (wo)man as a species-being within abstracted, de-ideologized, and de-conceptualized environmental frameworks: as a Heideggerian *being-in-the-world* (*in-der-Welt-sein*). The implications of this view are that once this lens is adopted, one is able to witness modes of oppression outside of their self-legitimating ideologies. Violence is laid both bare and apparent; the violence of our own society, the violence by which land is held, most specifically, comes into focus. Through the lens of Marx's historical materialism, we can view the human social landscape as minority *élite* groups oppressing majority underclass groups for the purpose, simply, of better resource-access. The reality of our own society thus becomes clearer: an economic and power *élite*—those beneficiaries and profiteers of capitalism—enforce a cultural hegemony by way of the multi-armed media-education-entertainment machine (a confluence of Althusser's ideological and repressive state apparatuses). A vast majority of the alienated, oppressed, and proletarianized poor capitulate themselves in service of an economic and social system which works *against* their best interests; serving, primarily, the profiteering and dominant *élite*—the bourgeoisies. Inside of this system, the vast majority are not free; they are alienated from themselves, the fruits of their own labor, and from the natural world itself. It is no surprise that a radical, counter-hegemonic stance exists which seeks to free the majority from such a yoke. And with the centers of militaristic power stationed within the ideological quagmire—the guns and power held, primarily, by the agents of the *élite* themselves—it stands to reason that education is thus the best weapon of the alienated and proletarianized masses; their only real recourse outside of often-suicidal armed revolution. Radical education helps to build the theoretical and revolutionary infrastructure which must be in place for any socialist praxis to be successful—even if that praxis must weight until capitalism collapses under its own weight.

As bell hooks wrote in *Teaching Critical Thinking*, an attempt towards the adoption of a de-ideologized world view "decolonize[s] our mind and the minds of our students" (28). Further implications of this view are bound up within the idea that the dominant modes of conception are not analogous to this view, but rather highly oppositional towards it. Along with the conception that there *might be* a de-ideologized way in which to view humanity comes the conception of the ubiquity of bourgeois ideology itself: the conception that, paradoxically, humanity is dominated by ideology—it reproduces its own servitude willingly, held inside of the most insidious of prisons: that of ideas and of the mind.

Part of the import of such critical pedagogues as Freire and hooks is that their existence, methodology, and impetus *define* the problem against which they are aligned; without them, we would not, quite as clearly, know against whom it is that we fight. And if, as these educators claim, and which we hold to be correct, there is a dominant educational system which recreates and perpetuates structures of oppression in both material and psychological arenas, then it behooves the oppressed—the ultimate victims of this system of education—to educate themselves regarding their own liberation. What the presence and work of critical educators such as hooks and Freire truly represents is, in part, the small but organized opposition to bourgeois education itself—that oppressive educational model which psychopathologizes its subjects into accepting their own willing oppression; an education which normalizes wage-servitude; and an educational system which in turn "subjectifies" its subjects, teaching them to recreate both the circumstances and situations

42

of their own oppression—indeed subjectivit itself,—thus ensuring the system's own longevity and discursive dominance.

In sum, several key points and self-evident premises seem to present themselves:

1. We currently exist within the epoch of (late) capitalism—a totalizing metabolic form which consists of both economically basic and ideologically superstructural aspects. Both the economic base and the ideological superstructure exist in a dialectical relationship with each other; their interplay is dynamic, and their effect is totalizing. As an epochal *produktionsweise*, capitalism legitimates itself—through the work of its legitimative ideologues—to the point where it is presented as evolutionarily natural, in humanity's best interest, and inescapable. As a productive mode, having taken shape from the ashes of feudal manorialism, capitalism has grown to dominate, in places like the U.S., the public and private educational apparatus. State curriculum and its pedagogical presentation disseminate and reproduce bourgeois cultural hegemony to such an extent that no alternative is visible.

2. The capitalist system can be viewed, however, through an historical-materialistic lens of class antagonism: within capitalism's organizational structure, a bipartite class system exists—a predatory class and a prey class, an oppressor class and an oppressed class. This dual-class analysis is intentionally reductive, yet it paints an adequate picture of the capitalist relationships of production, which entail, following Marx's theory of commodity fetishism ("Capital" 165), a base degradation of all personal relations, at their base, into economic relations. This economic relationship devolves into a two-tiered, topographical "those who exploit vs. those whom are exploited" structure. While the relationship between capitalism's "over" and "under" classes is inherently economic, as a radically counter-intuitive system for the exploited themselves, ideological machinations had to be employed to legitimate the oppressive economic relationship such that it appeared as a willing choice on the part of the exploited; a result of nature, naturalized, and arising from the best interest of the exploited.

3. If the oppressed, as exploited, are to continue to willingly participate with the reproduction of capitalism by way of its ideological legitimation and economic dominance, then there is

nothing left for them to do. If we, the oppressed, are happy with our oppression, then we must simply sit by and watch the architects of our fates design increasingly insidious and alienating circumstances, crises, and rationalities for us. However, if we, as the underclass, take an interest in our liberation, then there is indeed work to be done. Given that bourgeois ideology is taught to us by the multi-armed machinations of the repressive and ideological state apparatuses—by way of media, public education, and bourgeois political discourse—we must, following the Marxist line, seek our own liberation via our own means. We must *reclaim* our education. Sweeping, proletarian-originated, *educational* innovation must be a major focus of any communist praxis.

Assuming the above to be correct, education—radical education—is thus a major revolutionary tactic in the struggle against the proletarianizing force of bourgeois ideology. Our economic servitude to the bourgeois qua capitalist agenda—that agenda which ultimately serves the endemic profiteering *élite* class—exists inside of a legitimating and totalizing hegemony of bourgeois culture. Without an oppositional form of education through which we might seek our freedom, our future is bleak and without hope, as bourgeois ideology would like to have us, on some level, believe. But this is not the truth. If the work of such educators as hooks and Freire, and the writings of such theorists as Marx, Engels, Gramsci, and Lukács are to be accepted, then there is a way in which to remove ourselves—both ideologically and materially—from the yoke of economic servitude to which bourgeois production binds us: this way is the practice of mental freedom by way of education. Radical education enlightens us while at the same time freeing us. It teaches us that the seemingly-total grasp that bourgeois ideology has *might not be so total*—that it is neither permanent nor eternal. Through oppositional education, there is both freedom *and* hope. And through oppositional education we can begin to reclaim our relationship to the natural world—that world from which we have been alienated by both ideology and an exploitative economy.

CHAPTER III

Preconditions for the Articulation of a Theory of Communist Land Relations

The Preconditional Necessity
"Communism as a fully developed naturalism is humanism and as a fully developed humanism is naturalism" (Marx, 155).

In the previous chapter we covered several positions: we constructed a brief philosophical history of the bourgeoisies themselves, that we might better understand the ideology of the now-dominant social class. We focused on the work of one bourgeois philosopher in particular, David Hume, so that we might better understand the effort exercised in the purposeful crafting of ideology. We moved on to discuss how the *reason* of (wo)man has been coopted by bourgeois ideology in the epoch of capitalism, using, specifically, a critical framework. We then discussed how reason, once coopted by bourgeois ideology, becomes a mechanism of control—the machine of civil society. And finally we have discussed what we feel to be a key aspect of the reproduction of bourgeois ideology: the fact that it is delivered to the proletarian masses via the curricula of public education. And we have also suggested that education, radical-critical education, *must* be employed in the subversion of bourgeois ideology, as a revolutionary tactic. Thus, we have attempted to cover as many bases as possible, and to end our first chapter not in despair, but in hope.

In the present chapter, we seek to return to our central idea: that bourgeois land relations, as a function of bourgeois ideology—the nature-alienating aspect of ideology itself which severs the human organism from its natural world context—*must* be subverted, and in fact actively replaced, if the human species is to avoid the environmental and species-destruction meted out to it by the capitalist mode of production. We submit that we cannot escape ideology. Day-to-day, we swim within ideology as a fish within water—oblivious to its efforts, its effects, and the ways in which its currents shape both our ideation and our action. On this, Gramsci once noted that, "We are all conformists of some conformism or other, always man-in-the-mass or collective man" (324). Here, Gramsci follows the Kantian assertion, expanded upon by Marx, that (wo)man is first and foremost a species-being, a social animal. This is our hominid heritage. We submit again that we cannot escape ideology—that we cannot completely de-ideologize ourselves, for even this would occur from a position of ideology. The murky waters would quickly close in around us. What we can do, however, is attempt to subvert the dominant, destructive ideology and supplant it with an anti-ideology which is egalitarian, sustainable, and equitable. We can attempt to craft a conception of our political and environmental reality which is an accurate reflection of the world-as-it-is; we can base our ideas upon nature, upon preservationism, and upon the hopes that we might, by ennobling our own species, ennoble all life.

Following the Marxist classics, specifically the work of Marx himself, we assert that we must struggle to see the dominant ideology for what it is, and as clearly as possible; we must see the ideological water in which we swim and we must exercise our reason—our reason-reclaimed—to critique bourgeois ideology as *ruthlessly* as possible. When we engage in critique—ruthless, Marxist critique—we must do so as philosophers: as lovers of truth, and as the members of the oppressed. Why should we live in untruth? Why must we accept radically counterintuitive ideas, especially when, deep in our stomachs, we feel the falseness of the reality in which bourgeois ideology situates us? Why should we, as oppressed, blindly accept the proletarianizing ideology of our oppressors?

We aim, in the following pages, to build the framework for the eventuality of a *communist land relations* by discussing the *preconditions* which need to be met by an egalitarian, and communist, anti-ideology: one which is radically opposed to both exploitation and alienation, and one which properly situates the human species-being in a world which belongs, fairly, to all. Along these lines, what do we feel such a conception, such a communist anti-ideology, must entail? Firstly *communist land relations*—as a function of communist anti-ideology—*must* be critical; it must remain critical if it is to avoid falling into the trap of ossification. Hegel once claimed that the individual, the subject, "is the series of its actions" ("Philosophy of Right" 151). What this means to us is that at the base of all human structures, we have the individual subject—her series of actions; an existential result of her choices—and that these choices, and this unending series, predicates upon change itself. From this, we can take away two things: 1. The human subject is at the root of humanity itself.

Fundamentally, all human relations occur between subjects, and thus a land relationship which proclaims itself communist must itself acknowledge the fluid, changing nature of the individual and respond to such an atmosphere of change and subjectivity. It must withstand the test of time. Theoretical ossification does not serve the nature of the individual human subject, nor does it serve communist theory. 2. Given that the dynamic of change is assumed, critique *must* then be relied upon. We must remain critical to our changes, as they are not entirely within our control. We may not stay the same forever; life itself shows us this one glaring fact. Change is sometimes for the good. And it is sometimes for the bad. Only critique, ruthless critique, may remain to question the nature of change itself, as well as change's effects. And critique presupposes a criticizing subject; thus a communist land relations must acknowledge the subject, critique, and the *species-nature* of humanity itself. These, in our view, are the *initial* preconditions of a theory of communist land relations.

Secondly a theory of communist land relations must remain political: it must, conceptualizing (wo)man as a species-being, understand that the happenings of the polis—the organization of the social organism—predicate upon an history of power relations and of class antagonism. As a species being, as a primate with a history of social hierarchy, politics must be at the forefront of a communist land relations, and indeed communist anti-ideology at large. Communist anti-ideology is nothing other than the idea of pure egalitarianism: the antithesis of hierarchy and the dismantling of the domination of man by man. In this regard we wish to become not as history has shown us to be, but rather something better. We seek to become an animal which cares for the weakest among us, an animal which does not participate in genocides, and an animal whose social organization is based upon a true equality of all its constituent members. As an egalitarian animal, the necessity of a dominant class vanishes; indeed the concept of class itself vanishes altogether.

Thirdly, and finally, a theory of communist land relations, to meet the previous two conditions, must emerge from a perspective of dialecticalism: what we will call, for the purpose of land relations, a *tensioned identicalism* of organism and environment. "Thought and being are indeed distinct but they also form a unity," wrote the young Karl Marx ("Early Writings" 158), and it is within Marx's (Hegelian) conception of a unitive combination of opposites—sublative synthesis and the mutual destruction of oppositional forms—that we ground our theory of tensioned identicalism. We submit that it is *only* through a lens of dialectics that the world itself—inclusive of objective reality and perceiving subjects (opposites which indeed form a unity)—might be properly conceived. We, as species-being, view our world through a lens of polarity. Day and night, woman and man, good and evil, subject and object: we acknowledge that humanity has, historically, viewed its world through this lens of opposition. These are, however, analytical devices only—for in between man's dichotomous polarizing of his world exists, in actuality, many variegations. Kant himself acknowledged that it was indeed the antagonism between opposites—sociality and anti-sociality in his case— which drove civil society itself (44). However, we submit that in the midst of the perspective of antagonism lies a deeper truth which acknowledges both opposites and the shades of gray: a *unitive synthetic* which must acknowledge the oppositional nature of our world without simply reducing opposites into a reductive singularity or relying upon stark polarization. We seek to do justice to the complexity of reality itself and to the nature of change. We follow, here, the works of the great Marxist classics when we submit our term *tensioned identicalism* as a new terminological device. Further, we do not submit that the idea itself is new; again, only its relationship to land relations in regards to viewing the human subject and its natural world context as both distinct *yet* unified.

In the following sections, we will discuss the necessity of a theory of communist land relations to emerge as a critique—making a case for critical theory itself as essential to the fabric of this critique. We will discuss, briefly, the necessity for communist land relations to remain explicitly political, and we will make our case for the necessity of *tensioned identicalism* using the metaphysical lenses of three great thinkers: Karl Marx, Ludwig Wittgenstein, and Scott Warren.

A Case for the Necessity of Critique

A theory of communist land relations must remain critical. As humanity itself is ever-changing—and if the fascistic nature of bourgeois class rule is to be avoided, let alone subverted—critique itself must be the heart of all communist theory; communist land relations notwithstanding. And nowhere in the last hundred years of western philosophy does critique find a stronger home than in critical theory itself. Thus, in our view, a primary precondition for a theory of communist land relations— a communist environmental philosophy—is that it must, if it is to remain as critical as possible, align itself with the strongest body of contemporary radical critique in the last hundred years: critical theory itself. Critical theory is pertinent for the following three reasons:

1. Critical theory contains several radical epistemological and ontological assertions: (a) man is a species-being within an ontological totality, the fact of which is only obscured by man's own ignorance and a purposeful obfuscation on the part of the ideological superstructure; (b) the truth of reality, its totalized nature, is there to be realized, if one can but apply himself towards a critique of his own social-superstructural indoctrination, and the material reality which lies as its substratum; and (c) the social and productive forces which drive man in his relationship to both the world and society are antagonistic in nature—dialectical.

2. Critical theory is implicitly political: its critique of reality, and the basic focus of the project itself, inevitably turns towards the social organization of humans—towards economic relations, and towards the resultant superstructural ideology which legitimates, feeds, and furthers the economic-material base.

3. The critique of ideology—the ideology of Idealism, that bourgeois ideology which legitimates capitalist socio-economic structure, or the ideological-economical relationship itself—is inherently psychoanalytical. Critical theory rests upon a foundation of both Marx *and* Freud. The critique of human social relations—the base of all economic relations—is inherently a macro-critique of the social organism, of which man is but a discrete unit. In this regard, critical theory appears as the macro-psychoanalysis of capitalism, and of human socio-political organizations at large.

We aim to briefly elaborate upon these three aforementioned points in the following paragraphs of this section—citing where relevant, and hopefully articulating these points in such a way as to posit what we see as the import of critical theory itself: the ongoing investigation of the *unconcealed*, that unique aspect of reality which stands apart from the hyper-polarized subjective/objective conception of reality. This dialectical conception of the unconcealed reveals what is not *heimlich*, or home-like, but rather what is *unheimlich*, concealed, and uncanny: reality as a totality—bourgeois obfuscating ideology naught but a "self-incurred minority" (Kant 1) to which we unfortunately bow, unaware of the truth of the matter.

In opposition to the idea that man either exists as a solipsistic being unto himself, the objective reality of the "out there" being entirely "in here" (a radical subjectivity) or that he essentially does not exist apart from his quantification inside of an entirely objective reality (a radical objectivity), critical theory maintains the ontological assertion that man exists as a unity of the subject-object inside of a wholistic totality, amongst antagonistic forces which create a sort of dialectical tension between the subject-object, thus furthering man's evolution and growth.

Signs of "man as a species-being" and "antagonistic tension" began to emerge in Kant, within two essays in specific: *Idea for a Universal History with a Cosmopolitan Purpose* and *What is Enlightenment?* Kant noted that:

> The history of mankind can be seen, in the large, as the realization of Nature's secret plan to bring forth a perfectly constituted state as the only condition in which the capacities of mankind can be fully developed, and also bring forth that external relation among states which is perfectly adequate to this end (7).

Kant also asked, "Is it reasonable to assume a purposiveness in all the parts of nature and to deny it to the whole?" (6). Or, in other words, if nature itself is seen to have purposiveness in its doings—the totality of the natural world doing as it does for its own purposeful ends—is it not folly then to assume man to be a completely irrational species, guided only by its whims? While Kant seemed to envision man working, as an organ of Nature, towards its own enlightened and harmonious ends, even if we reject the premise that man has purpose, the reality of man as an organismic being—as an animal species evolving along its own animalistic path towards the purpose of, as Lukács put it, "positing, producing, and reproducing oneself" (14)—persists. If we reject the idealistic bourgeois claims that nature itself exists *for* us, and if we adopt a stance that we exist in totality with nature as one of its many "species-beings," we begin to emerge into the mindset of what we see as the fundamental ontological claim of critical theory itself, and indeed a foundation of all communist land relations: man is an animal.

Kant asked:

> [...] are we not rather to suppose that Nature here follows a lawful course in gradually lifting our race from the lower levels of animality to the highest level of humanity, doing this by her own secret art, and developing in accord with her law all the original gifts of man in this apparently chaotic disorder? (6)

Kant posited that we can know this truth, if we but "dare to be wise" (1). Hints of man's antagonistic nature—a glimpse into the dialectical perspective of reality—began to also emerge with Kant. As mentioned earlier, he seemed to posit antagonism as the creative force of man's evolution: "The means employed by Nature to bring about the development of all the capacities of men is their antagonism in society, so far as this is, in the end, the cause of a lawful order among men" (3). The antagonistic forces, for Kant, manifest as man's inherent unsociability alongside man's desire to exist in society—his sociability. But here we see, in theoretical nascency, the dialectic at work: forces acting in opposition to create a type of synthesis (which itself stands in opposition to an opposing force, creating new synthesis ad infinitum). This important beginning of what political philosopher Scott Warren called "dialectical theory" is evidenced by its development in Lukács, who wrote that the dialectical method holds a "methodological supremacy" (9) in regards to both epistemology and ontology.

As both communist theory and critical theory's primary, foundational thinkers, Marx and Engels did much to carry forward the examination of man's social antagonism towards an analysis of political relations—the antagonism which exists between those who seek to direct and those whom are directed. What takes root in Kant as the concept of "alien guidance " (54) is taken up more fully by Marx and Engels in *The German Ideology* as an examination of class antagonism and of (proletarian) man's enslavement "under a power alien to [him] [...] *the world market*" (27). Marx and Engels, from the extant fabric of contemporaneous socialist thought, focused their project on the establishment of international communism—that aim which seems to give critical theory its driving force: the liberatory project of man's own freedom from the domination of other men and from productive forces which have, as Lukács put it, "escaped their control" (15).

The implicitly political nature of critical theory began with the work of Marx and Engels, who realigned philosophy as an investigation of man-in-the-world. In *The German Ideology* we read that, "The first premise of human history is, of course, the existence of living human individuals. Thus the first fact to be established is the physical organization of these individuals and their consequent relation to the rest of nature" (7). Thus began the modern focus on man-as-animal, and his organizational-metabolic nature—the essence of which is inherently historico-political. Following man's antagonistic inner-nature, an investigation of the antagonism of social classes—oppressors and oppressed—is naturally entailed. "Man must be viewed in his real historical activity and existence" (155); or, in other words, the folly of our myopic thinking in regards to only ourselves must be dropped: we must conceptualize ourselves correctly as existing world-historically. From this accurate conceptualization will most naturally follow an investigation of human social organization, of domination and submission, and of material relations—the realm of material production. In ascertaining an accurate world-historical situation of humanity—its vast majority oppressed, controlled, and ideologized by a dominant minority—the philosopher, as a lover of wisdom and truth, seems most naturally led to an examination of the liberation of the oppressed majority. While the project might be seen as inherently utilitarian, there does seem to be some positive ethical quality—some basic goodness, if such a thing could be said to exist—in busying oneself with the project of the liberation of the oppressed from the yoke of the oppressors.

The political, for Marx and Engels—the obvious thrust of the communist project—is thus a necessary axis around which to center one's work. In *The Holy Family*, Marx and Engels asked, "If *political* movements *have social significance*, how can political interests appear '*insignificant*' in comparison with their own social significance?" (122). Far from being an insignificant facet of social or theological investigation, the examination of the political takes on an importance of Kantian measure: an expression of man's species-goal to work himself up "from the lowest barbarity to the highest skill and mental perfection [which] thereby work[s] himself up to happiness (so far as it is possible on earth)" (Kant 3).

Heidegger, in his *Origin of the Work of Art*, noted that "All works have this thingly part. What would they be without it?" (3). He went on, later, to ask, "What happens here? What is at work in the work? [...] [The] entity emerges into the unconcealedness of its being" (36). What Heidegger seemed to posit was the world-historical nature of a thing: its thingness as an aspect of the totality of reality—that *unheimlich* nature which stands as a unique interpretation of the dialectical tension which exists between the individual *perceiving* subject and the *perceived* object; that essence of the thing which is neither entirely objective nor completely subjective. This unique nature of the *unfamiliar*—Heidegger here resurrected the Greek term *aletheia*—is important to critical theory in that it further develops the idea of the totality, of what-is. Heidegger wrote that since the time of Aristotle, "Agreement with what *is* has long been taken to be the essence of truth" (36-37). The nature of "what *is*" is important in that it situates the individual critical theorist—and ruthless critique in general—in a unique place to both ascertain and conceptualize an accurate (material) view of reality: able to ascertain the world-historical situation of (wo)man, to ascertain the nature of the socio-economic relations of (wo)man, and to conceptualize a framework which truthfully pictures reality as a the interchange and evolution of human relations, oppressions, and organizations.

Heidegger's focus on *aletheia*, what Freud might call the *unheimlich*, further refined (and fed) critical theory in such a way as to suggest that our primary conceptions of reality rested upon our (false) conceptions themselves. "Art is truth setting itself to work" (39) and such is the world. When viewed incorrectly, the world is viewed from the perspective of ideology which is largely, if not entirely, in service of the bourgeoisies. Artwork, for example, might be taken as a representation of beauty; however, social notions of beauty might rest upon bourgeois characteristics of material wealth, perfection of form, lasciviousness of culture, and so on. If we perceive and conceptualize art—and, further, the world—through the unconscious lens of bourgeois culture, then we see the world as the bourgeoisie intend us to, and we take part in the reproduction of the world after *their* image: to be grasped, attained, conquered, and held. However, if we are able, as Heidegger suggested, to somehow suspend our enmeshment within ideology, if we are able to see a thing as it actually is, we are able to grasp its fleeting unconcealedness of being—its truth. Extrapolated out to a proper conception/perception of the world, the unconcealedness of the totality becomes a thing-view which reveals itself as a unity, its *tensioned* dialectical (total) nature revealed in its unique existence as a subject-object—inextricable from the perceiving individual—yet perceptible and conceptualizable above superstructural ideology: a transcendent totality—being as being.

Recognition of this totality is, in our view, inherently psychoanalytical. Given that the individual must himself conceptualize reality in this way as a subject-object, he himself is intimately involved in its conception/perception. Freud, in his *Introductory Lectures on Psychoanalysis*, wrote that, "it is a predisposition of human nature to consider an unpleasant idea untrue, [it is then] easy to find arguments against it. Society thus brands what is unpleasant as untrue, denying the conclusions of psychoanalysis with logical and pertinent arguments" (17). This predisposition, in our view, extends to the propensity of man to fall back on ideology when perceiving/conceiving the world. If one is to truly ascertain the truth of the world-historical and the world-political, one must be willing to acknowledge the antagonistic nature of the social reality in which one participates and of which one is a part. Any white-washed conception of the world through bourgeois ideology presents a false picture of the world, and this, to us, seems to be the greatest contribution of both Freud and Heidegger to critical theory itself: the ability to recognize, perceive, and conceptualize a reality which is in absolute agreement with *what is*. As in psychoanalysis, if the truth of an individual's psychology—in efforts to work towards its health and betterment—is to be fully ascertained, its full truth, both its pleasantness and its unpleasantness, must be perceived and recognized. The same goes for a true conception of the world, and of world-historical circumstances. Critical theory, when seen in this light, *appears to be psychoanalysis extrapolated out to the macrocosm of the social totality*, in that it positively conceptualizes the *epochal* nature of modes of production by examining their negative aspects—hidden, repressed, or suppressed forces such as ideology which, in actuality, and while not discussed, are indeed quite formative-reproductive. And in this regard, the application of critical theory to the conceptualization of a theory of communist land relations first takes root as a type of psychoanalysis of bourgeois land relations—its critique aimed at social and global self-betterment.

In sum, the general *weltanschauung* of critical theory itself is one which sets its sights on a perception/conception of reality which lies outside of the legitimating and perpetuating bourgeois ideological superstructure which, as it does, strengthens, enforces and furthers extant (bourgeois) economics. And while this purpose—of a correct perception of reality—might be shared/claimed by every philosophical school since the pre-Socratics, critical theory's unique contribution to communist theory at large seems to lie in its relevance to our current world-historical circumstances, as well as to a commitment to continually ascertain and re-ascertain the dialectically evolving nature of these circumstances. It sets its sights on a *critique ad infinitum*. As mentioned earlier, with the changing face of economic and social factors so must we, apparently and continually, reevaluate our positions. This is a nail in the coffin for ideology, which seems to want to ossify truth into a form which does not agree with the what-is. And this is the primary pitfall for communist theory at large: ossification to an almost religious degree. As Lukács noted, "At every stage of social evolution each economic category reveals a definite relation between men. This relation becomes conscious and conceptualized" (15). By focusing on this conceptualization, critical theory offers what we see as a correct ascertainment of the unconcealedness of reality: one which is inherently political, in that its efforts are directed towards human liberation from bourgeois oppression, and one which is inherently self-corrective—psychoanalytical on the scale of the societal macrocosm.

Dialectics and Politics

"For an answer which cannot be expressed the riddle too cannot be expressed. The riddle does not exist" (Wittgenstein 107).

"[G]ive up your abstraction and at the same time you abandon your question. [...] Do not think, do not ask me any questions, for as soon as you think and ask questions your abstraction from the existence of nature and man becomes meaningless" (Marx "Early Writings" 166).

We submit that a response to bourgeois capitalism—a response to bourgeois ideology itself—must by necessity be political. A counter-capitalism which lies upon a blindness to the political (and violent) nature of capitalism itself has the potential to end up as a type of reproductive reaction. "The proletariat needs state power," wrote Lenin, "the centralized organization of force, the organization of violence, for the purpose of crushing the resistance of the exploiters and for the purpose of leading the great mass of the population—the peasantry, the petty bourgeoisie, the semi-proletarians—in the work of organizing socialist economy" (288). Ignorance of the political nature of the capitalist mode of production—crafting a revolution on such a blindness—might have us believing that we can, for example, *spend* our way out of capitalism. It might have us imagine that through such an avenue as ethical spending, we might subvert the great and totalized socio-economic machine. But this is of course false. And this falsity, in our view, rests upon a view that is inherently dichotomous—a digital view that would have us look only to the discrete, without a conception of the totality itself. No, a proper response to capitalism, if it is to be effective at all, must be critical, political, *and* it must entail such a theoretical framework as to properly conceptualize the totalizing nature of capitalism, and politics, at large. This framework must be *dialectical* in nature—a framework which properly conceptualizes the nature of change, the nature of structures, and the *unitive synthetic* nature of reality itself. A view which entails what we aim to call, regarding land relations, a *tensioned identicalism*.

To conceptualize such a dialectic we must of course return to Marx. However, in our view, to achieve here a fuller view of Marx, whose arguments against the abstractive, and divisive, nature of thought took shape early in his life, one must also adopt the positivistic and contra-linguistic lens of Ludwig Wittgenstein—the great 20th century philosopher and logician. No two thinkers might seem, prima facie, as disparate in their theories as Ludwig Wittgenstein and Karl Marx. However, upon closer examination, we begin to notice a striking number of similarities in their work concerning both the limits of language and the synthetic nature of the subject-object relationship. Indeed, we will attempt to make the claim that without the linguistic-philosophical lens of Ludwig Wittgenstein, without a conceptualization which does not reach beyond the limits of language itself, any sort of accurate conceptualization of reality, of bourgeois ideology, or of political theory will fall flat—doomed to ideological quagmire. Simply put: language, by virtue of its *signifying* quality, can never actually *be* the thing which it signifies; it can only signify. And, as such, any linguistic conceptualization of a component of reality will simply fall apart at a certain level of analysis, its truth evaporating in favor of a nonlinguistic conception which can never be signified.

Ideology itself works upon us in many forms, but as a collection of (false) ideas, it takes as its corporeal form the body of language within our minds themselves. In this way, ideology creates within us a *false consciousness*. Ideas may exist, ultimately, beyond linguistic signification; but they present themselves to us cloaked in words, in a language which sits like a skin upon the unconscious. And linguistic signification itself, a categorizational device, purposefully separates totality into discrete units; it is designed to do so. But far from reductive synthesizing, what we seek to emphasize as a necessary precondition of communist push-back, a precondition for any sound theory of communist land relations, is the idea that a view which encompasses totality—one which, for example, properly conceptualizes the totalizing base-superstructural nature of capitalism—must at the same time acknowledge the parts while comprehending the unity. Both the reductive-unitive perspective and the categorizing-discrete view do not adequately conceptualize the reality of capitalism, or reality itself for that matter. We are then left to argue for a dialectical view which acknowledges the unity of things while also acknowledging the ontological-metaphysical tension between them.

While separated by history, both Wittgenstein and Marx seemed to agree that the central source of philosophical—and political—confusion is linguistic-abstractive in nature. In his early manuscripts, Marx stated that, "your question is itself a product of abstraction. Ask yourself how you arrive at that question. Ask yourself whether your question does not arise from a point of view to which I cannot reply because it is a perverted one" (166). Similarly, what Wittgenstein seemed to state as the

56

driving thesis of his *Tractatus Logico-Philosophicus* was that: "What can be said at all can be said clearly; and whereof one cannot speak thereof one must remain silent" (27).

Both Marx and Wittgenstein seemed to also agree on the metaphysical subject-object unity: a *tensioned* position which entails many powerful ontological implications—stretching out into the epistemological, the political, the psychological, and beyond. Wittgenstein made his case clear in the midst of his fifth propositional elaboration, by stating:

> [5.621] The world and life are one. [5.63] I am my world. (The microcosm.) [5.631] The thinking, presenting subject; there is no such thing. [...] [5.632] The subject does not belong to the world but is a limit of the world (89).

Wittgenstein elaborated by stating that any complete definition of his world must necessarily include a definition of himself, the observer and experiencer of his world (89). Or, in other words, Wittgenstein saw no distinction between the metaphysical subject and object—both of them existing as a type of synthetic whole (dialectical tension notwithstanding). We cannot know *ourselves* outside of *our world*. Marx elaborated his position on the subject-object dynamic early in his career, as evidenced by his work in the *Early Writings*:

> Though man is a unique individual—and it is just his particularity which makes him an individual, a really *individual* communal being—he is equally the whole, the ideal whole, the subjective existence of society as thought and experienced. [...] Thought and being are indeed *distinct* but they also form a unity (Marx 158).

Marx, here, recognized the distinctness of both subjective thought and objective being, the unification (as *aufhebung*) of the two heretofore disparate realms of substance are essential to his philosophical, and political, position—a view which entails a *sublation* of seeming opposites. In our view, the immanence of the subject/object gives Marx the metaphysical impetus to propose his entire system of social change. Idealistic substance dualism, for example—an ontological irreconcilability between the metaphysical subject and object—leaves an exit for those who might see fit to ignore worldly injustice and the dominance of capital in lieu of heavenly rewards. Philosopher Scott Warren elaborated on the nature and reason of a unified subject-object position by stating that, "[b]ecause of the philosophy of identity, consciousness does not simply 'know' the object, it must directly be the object" (56).

In this section, we aim to explore two key areas of similarity between the positions of Wittgenstein and Marx, as mediated by Warren: 1. the metaphysical subject-object unity; and 2. the resultant limits of language—as well as the limit of these limits. We view Wittgenstein's position on subject-object unity to be, essentially, a restatement of Marx's positions, but without a key aspect which is only added into the equation by Scott Warren's astute perspectives: an acknowledgement of the dialectical, and metaphysical, *tension* that exists between subject and object. While Wittgenstein's subject-object unity offered to us a type of solipsism of *pure realism*, of sorts, we feel that he fell short of addressing a self-evident reality of our existence as a species-being, as well the relationship of dialectical inextricability of the metaphysical subject and object. Realizing that we apply language as an analytical device in efforts of understanding our reality, a complete unification of the subject and object negates the dialectical tension that exists between these two metaphysical positions, as well as the helical interrelation and *change* that both subject and object enact upon each other. In essence, we hope to present the perspectives of Marx, tempered with the explanations of Warren, as providing a fuller example of the truth of the Wittgensteinian matter: that both subject and object do indeed represent a unity which borders on solipsism, but that this solipsism is qualified by a nuanced dialectical relationship—a tension—between both subject and object. Further, we would like to explore some of the Wittgensteinian limits of language that result from a subject-object unity, and raise several questions in regards to the inefficacy of remaining silent upon things about which, according to Wittgenstein, one cannot speak.

> The dialectic of subject and object now emerges in a new light. Its locus is man the creator and creature of nature. As 'living being' he is subject, and as 'embodied being' he is object. Man now appears as the subject-object (Warren 56).

Wittgenstein emphasized that the metaphysical subject "does not belong to the world but is a limit of the world" (89). Or, in other words, what philosophy had previously asserted to be the subject—the individual experiencer—is not, in any way, divorced nor ontologically distinct from its world of experience: experience and experiencer are one. And as a "limit" of the world, the subject is simply a limit of all possible

58

experiences: a locality which contains and limits the total reality—
something of a bubble of experience. We cannot, for example, know
certain things about the world directly through our experience: subject-
as-limit prevents us from experiencing, presently, an event on the other
side of the world.

Scott Warren elaborated on the subject-object relationship by
clarifying that:

> If one accepts the dialectic of subject and object, then one
> approaches the understanding of anything in terms of the
> relations between subject and object, since the nature of
> something lies neither inside it nor outside it alone, but in relation
> between inner and outer, subjectivity and objectivity (54).

Or, in other words, consideration of the subject qua object and the object
qua subject might be something of a gross overstatement: it does not
recognize the implicit *dialectical tension* and complexity of the truth of their
relationship. Wittgenstein emphasized that, "The sense of the world must
lie outside the world. In the world everything is as it is and happens as it
does happen. In it there is no value—and if there were, it would be of no
value" (105). Or, in other words, the (illusory) distinctions between
subject and object are self-evident to the experience of the singled-out
subject: however any sense of their dialectical tension is a transcendent
value which lies outside of logic. But is this simply sophism on
Wittgenstein's part, or are there very real logical structures about which
we can speak, concerning the relationship between subject and object?

Wittgenstein hints at this dialectical tension by claiming, on the
one hand, that:

> [6.373] The world is independent of my will. [6.374] Even if
> everything we wished were to happen, this world would only be,
> so to speak, a favour of fate, for there is no logical connexion
> between will and world, which would guarantee this, and the
> assumed physical connexion itself could not again will (104);

and, on the other hand, that:

> [5.63] I am my world. (The microcosm.) [...] [5.633] Where in the
> world is a metaphysical subject to be noted? [5.64] Here we see
> that solipsism strictly carried out coincides with pure realism. The

> I in solipsism shrinks to an extensionless point and there remains
> the reality co-ordinated with it (90).

Wittgenstein claimed three things which exhibit a fair amount of tension:
(1) The "I" and the world are one; (2) the world, however, is independent
of the will of the "I"; and (3) the independent, synthesized world-"I"
dialectic is, for the individual, all there is—"not the man, not the human
body or the human soul [...] but the metaphysical subject, the limit" (90).
Presented as a dialectic, Wittgenstein's points indeed beg a small amount
of further elaboration. They carry the weight, as Wittgenstein might have
wanted, of self-evidency; however there still remains a degree of
explanation needed, in our view.

For Wittgenstein, the unity of the metaphysical subject-object is a
unity of solipsism-pure realism: we, as the individual subject, cannot
escape our identification with the objects of our experience. We cannot
know ourselves outside of ourselves. The objects within our field of
subjective experience *belong to* and are identified with our subjective field
of experience. And since we cannot escape our own perspectives, we
cannot empirically claim that they—the objects—have an objective
existence outside of our perception. But, while evidently true—we cannot
escape our personal subjective experience to establish autonomous
objectivity—both the determinate nature of man, man as an objective
being to other men, our dialogical relationships, and so on, present an
ontological solipsism which does not align with scientific objectivity. And
here Marx might offer a fuller vision of Wittgenstein's terse aphorisms.
Scott Warren emphasized that:

> Marx's point is that any being which is not objective, nor has a
> real object, is a non-being. Otherwise we recur to a kind of
> ontological solipsism. In this sense the dialectic truly becomes
> concrete and total. For if 'I have an object, this object has me for
> its object,' which is to say, the object itself has a subjective
> character (54).

Wittgenstein might respond that there is no way to infer the reverse-
perspective of the subject-object unitive relationship, however we are in
agreement here with both Marx and Warren that the character of this
ontological solipsism, as articulated by Wittgenstein, is in need of this sort
of qualification, else it has the capability to descend into a quagmiric
solipsism—a regressus in/ad infinitum. In the words of Shiva Rahbaran,

"this sort of self-reflexive observation could [...] lead to solipsism and regressus ad infinitum and instead of liberating the individual, plunging him into an even more self-destructive entrapment" (xvi).

The tensioned unity of subject-object, which Marx puts forth as a predicate to the rest of his political philosophy, his conception of the capitalist historical phenomenon, can be recapitulated in his statement that, "Thought and being are indeed *distinct* but they also form a unity. *Death* seems to be a harsh victory of the species over the individual and to contradict their unity; but the particular individual is only a *determinate species-being* and as such he is mortal" (158-159). In contrast to Wittgenstein's view that death is "not an event of life. Death is not lived through" (106), Marx here takes the pervasive, ubiquitous, and daily example of the death of others to illustrate the dialectical tension between our apparent subject-object unity, and the larger objective reality to which we all indeed belong. While Wittgenstein here might have argued that our idea borders on non sequitur, and that his argument is strictly from the stance of individual epistemology, we feel that Marx here offers a fuller, more qualified explanation of the subject-object unity in the face of the seeming fallacy of solipsism, when considering our relationship to others. Following Kant, Marx here emphasizes that we are a species-being first, an individual second, and that our unity of individual experience is also bound up within our unity as a species: we do not exist as solo operators within a slice of time, but rather as part of a diverse, yet homogeneous, collective—of which we are but a unit.

Scott Warren further emphasized the qualified subject-object unity (qualified by the tension of the dialectical unity and species-nature) by stating that:

> The reason that this recovery of the sensuous objectivity of man and reality does not lead to either empiricism or simple naturalism is that 'man is not merely a natural being.' He is also human and as such is a subjective natural being. Therefore man is a being with self-consciousness (a species-being) who expresses himself in both thought and nature (55).

Or, in other words, the over-simplified solipsistic position does not take into account a reality of human interaction—social and political interaction—which thus refutes any polarized, radical objectivity or radical subjectivity (solipsism). Thought and being, subject and object, the I and the world, form a sublated, interactional dialectic—an identicalized back-and-forth of interaction and transformation which represents both a profound unity of subject and object, but also pays regard to the extant dialectical tension which shapes and gives purpose to the back-and-forth itself: *tensioned identicalism.*

"Whereof one cannot speak, thereof one must remain silent*"* *(*Wittgenstein 108*).*
"My own existence is a social activity" (Marx 158).

Upon an initial reading of Ludwig Wittgenstein's *Tractatus Logico-Philosophicus*, his political leanings might at first appear disinterested, if not only mildly sympathetic towards the radical left in general. Indeed, journalist David Stern noted philosopher Gavin Kitching's sentiments that Wittgenstein was himself a philosopher who "'showed virtually no interest in conventional political activity,' famous for writing that 'philosophy [...] leaves everything as it is'" (1). However, Stern went on to state explicitly that "[Wittgenstein] is said to have described himself as 'a communist at heart'" (Stern 1). Wittgenstein's communist leanings are an interesting juxtaposition to the thoughts of his mentor, Bertrand Russell, who stated that, "For my part, I think the theoretical tenets of Communism are false, and I think its practical maxims are such as to produce an immeasurable increase of human misery [...] I have always disagreed with Marx" (Russell 1). Might it have been that Wittgenstein's philosophy led him to a stance of inaction; a place of remaining silent about the things upon which he could not speak? Did political theory relegate itself to a system of ethics or aesthetics for Wittgenstein, thus rendering it unspeakable? In his *Tractatus*, Wittgenstein stated plainly in 6.421 that, "It is clear that ethics cannot be expressed. Ethics is transcendent. (Ethics and aesthetics are one.)" (105). If Wittgenstein indeed saw political theory as a form of ethics—a theory upon which we, as tensioned subject-object identities, could not logically speak given its inherent illogicality and thus unspeakability—what does this then say for those who in fact usurp Wittgenstein's model, bringing political theory into the realm of the speakable; thus bending the transcendent to the dictates of the immanent, warping unspeakable ethics into a fashion as to prop up oppressive dictatorships and variegated social structures predicated upon human bondage? In the face of these individuals, are we to remain silent—bending to the supposed limits of language?

There are, apparently, many ways to read Ludwig Wittgenstein's *Tractatus Logico-Philosophicus* as evidenced by the manifold ways in which the *Tractatus* is applied to political philosophy, linguistic theory, and metaphysics: manifold both in its application and its analysis. "There are commentators who see Wittgenstein as a Burkean conservative, a radical democrat, a Pyrrhonian skeptic, and a nihilist" (Moore 1113). These views, obviously, stand both in contradiction and contradistinction to one another—leading one to wonder which understanding is the most correct, if any. In regard to this confusion, the abstruse nature of the text itself may be to blame: Wittgenstein himself states that:

> My propositions are elucidatory in this way: he who understands me finally recognizes them as senseless, when he has climbed out through them, on them, over them. (He must so to speak throw away the ladder, after he has climbed up on it. He must surmount these propositions; then he sees the world rightly" (108).

Or, in other words, Wittgenstein's analysis of (logical) thought qua language is intended to be utilized to transcend itself: the message of the text is essentially, in our view, that while we can form an accurate *signification* of reality by utilizing linguistic thinking, the propositions—the linguistic descriptors themselves—are inherently senseless. In this way, while our words form a picture of reality that either: (a) accurately represents reality (truth), or (b) inaccurately represents reality (falsity), the words themselves are only terminological devices which we have heaped upon an essentially *termless* reality. Or, in other words, all philosophy falls apart outside of the mind of (wo)man: the world is as it is, and the ceaseless bickering over semantics, definitions, and linguistic problems represent arguments over ways in which reality is pictured. Wittgenstein seems to say that the words are ours; reality belongs to itself alone, existing only as a myriad of sense impressions.

As Wittgenstein put it, so eloquently succinct, "The riddle does not exist" (107). The problem we have with reality is our own. And further, all philosophical problems are reduced to bickering over representations. And arguments of ethics and "oughts" take a turn towards the transcendental, for Wittgenstein. As a representation of a sense of the world, ethics "must lie outside of the world" (105). Indeed, "Ethics is transcendental. (Ethics and aesthetics are one.)" (105). As an example of an "ought"—a system of macro-societal ethics and structure—political theory could be seen, in a Wittgensteinian sense, to be a form of ethics. Thus, represented in the form of a Celarent (EAE-1) syllogism:

1. No Ethics can be expressed.

2. All Political Theory is Ethics.
3. No Political Theory is expressible.

However, this presents a rather large problem for the existence of political theory. Moore addressed this problem in his article *Wittgenstein, value pluralism and politics* (2010) by articulating the essentially ambiguous nature of Wittgenstein's political implication, thus refuting all interpretations of Wittgenstein as a conservative, a democrat, a nihilist, *et cetera ad nauseum.* As Moore noted:

> Thus, instead of the traditional philosophical goal of political cooperation bounded by moral obligations that all rational actors must acknowledge and obey, and instead of a mere Hobbesian ceasefire among mutually hostile parties, we could achieve a kind of layered pluralism, in which individuals and societies cooperate in a wide variety of ways, for a variety of reasons, some resting on moral duties, others on support for institutions, and yet others on various kinds of self-interest (1132).

Moore summed up that, while we may not like to rest in such ambiguity, "that may be the world in which we find ourselves" (1132). Thus, that Wittgenstein proclaimed a type of political ambiguity is something of an understatement. Political Theory, as a strong example of an "ought," an Ethics, lies beyond the world. It is an indication of a direction of human will, and for Wittgenstein the world itself is "independent of [human] will" (104). Thus the world, as "the totality of facts" (29), does not entail "oughts"; it does not entail a particular system to which we should adhere in regard to our macro-societal structure, to our forms and methods of governance, and to our economic policy. The world itself does not entail political theory. And thus political theory, for Wittgenstein, is not a fact. But is this the case?

We may, in historical analysis, represent regime and polity as fact, although devoid of sense and "ought." Political theory, and the various terminological devices applied to the study of regime, does then exist as a sort of retrospective fact. We may conduct an analysis of history, and we may construct propositions based upon historical fact—and this necessarily entails analyses of the ways in which societies govern, organize into regimes, and conduct economies. And this, in our view, falls under the category of proposition and fact as long as we do not derive sense from the fact. Moral "oughts" must not be inferred from our analysis.

64

Thus it seems that, for Wittgenstein, political theory *could* exist only as historical analysis; but never as inference of the ways in which we *should* socio-politically organize. But does this not seem a small bit confusing? We may analyze the facts of history, thus correctly picturing our world, but we might never draw sense from the past; never formulate an "ought" for the ways in which we should, based upon analysis of past mistakes, better organize? From this, it follows that there does exist a type of ethics, a type of political instinct. From these apparent inconsistencies (possibly in our own understanding), and following our earlier syllogism, a new (Barbara AAA-1) syllogism might then be drawn:

1. All Ethics can be expressed retrospectively.
2. All Political Theory is Ethics.
3. All Political Theory can be expressed retrospectively (as historical analysis).

But, here we have something of a contradiction: political theory both *can* and *cannot* be expressed. We see an important problem here: in the contradiction lies the possibility for the existence of an inference of "ought"; the formulation of a type of political Ethics. However, Wittgenstein asserted that "All inference takes place a priori" (68) and that the "events of the future cannot be inferred from those of the present" (68). If we follow our logic, we see the futility, according to Wittgenstein, of stating political "oughts" a priori. There might be at least one problem with our line of thinking, however: for Wittgenstein, the world being essentially non-linguistic, we might be drawing an incorrect connection between the concepts of "doing history" and "doing political theory." Perhaps they are completely separate things; or perhaps political theory reduces into history. If Wittgenstein is correct in his presentation of the *Tractatus*, it may just.

However, we feel the analyses of history to be variegated enough to draw distinctions between the "kinds" of history that we "do." In the analyzing of scientific fact, in the saying only of "what can be said, *i.e.* the propositions of natural science" (108), we must invariably come to an analysis of political regime. And it is within this area of analysis and exploration that the a posteriori inferences of political theory begin to show themselves.

In the discussion of the propositions of natural science, it is not a great leap to speak about living organisms learning from pain, *i.e.* we place my hand on a hot stove, become burned, and learn (infer) to not do so in the future. We may not be able to infer whether a stove is hot or not, but we can reasonably infer that all hot stoves must necessarily cause us pain—this is a proposition of scientific fact regarding the study of pain. It is in this regard that the heretofore a priori inferences of political theory present themselves within our analysis of Wittgensteinian logic, thus becoming a type of a posteriori inference—a presentation of course-correction based upon an historical analysis of regime, economy, and so on. If, upon an analysis of historical polities and regimes, we can conclude that a specific type of regime equates to higher or lower levels of pain—quantified through an analysis of human deaths, animal deaths, acres of environmental destruction, and so on—might we not be able to draw the conclusion that some regimes are better than others? Might we conduct a type of a posteriori political theory which posits an "ought" based off of an historical analysis? In this way, would we thus bring political theory, as an Ethics, into the realm of the scientific and the concrete? Does then a new syllogism emerge (Darii AII-1)?

1. All pain causes organismic aversion.
2. Some forms of regime (following a political theory) cause pain.
3. Some regimes cause organismic aversion.

Following this logic, we are led to disagree with Moore, who earlier called for a type of value pluralism in regards to political theory. To be sure, there will always exist a plurality of opinion, theory, and value; however, utilizing logic, and following Wittgenstein's own exhortations, we can be led to privilege some values over others, some political theories over others, and some regimes over others. And while it seems that the orthodox Tractarian logic might, upon first glance, lead us to a form of radical political ambiguity, the possibility of (logically) arriving at an "ought" in regard to regime, polity, and governance becomes quite clear upon a close examination of the logic itself.

> "Human objects are never direct natural objects, and human sense is never immediate, given sensibility. Marx is no empiricist. The human being never confronts directly either objective or subjective nature. The relation is always a mediated one; human nature is a mediation of subject and object, which is to say, the process of its own genesis as the synthetic process of social labor and the conscious process of history" (Warren 55).

In closing, we assert that Wittgenstein may indeed be used politico-theoretically, and that, further, his perspectives on the limits of language are *essential* to a fuller understanding of dialectics themselves. We feel that the qualifications of Wittgenstein's linguistic theories which we have presented by way of both Marx and Warren add a fuller, political dimension to Wittgenstein's work: allowing us to tease out the implicit politics of works such as the *Tractatus Logico-Philosophicus* in such a way as to make them workable. Wittgenstein's openly communist sentiment (a "communist at heart") presents the reality of his views which may not be initially apparent within his work. Wittgenstein was a powerfully observant philosopher; his views would lend a great amount of support to any political theory—especially towards those to which he was sympathetic.

While Wittgenstein's subtextual perspectives might have been inherently communist, the overtness of such an association was likely, if not purposefully, obfuscated. In our view, given the deep similarity between Marx and Wittgenstein's ontological and linguistic theories, the room yet exists for an incredible amount of crossover. Our suggestion is that communist theory—and Marxist theory in general—should reclaim its implicit—and early—ontological focus, its implicit environmental focus, and its acceptance of abstract-linguistic emptiness; that it would be better served by an acknowledgement of that "feeling of the world as a limited whole" (107.) Whatever the level of crossover yet to be drawn, we are certain that remaining silent about such things as political ethics, the destruction endemic to the capitalist mode of production, and bourgeois mental enslavement by way of ideology is not only inherently incorrect; it allows for debased and fascistic views to arise uncontested.

CHAPTER IV

Conclusion

Aufheben

"It compels all nations, on pain of extinction, to adopt the bourgeois mode of production; it compels them to introduce what it calls civilization into their midst, i.e., to become bourgeois themselves. In a word, it creates a world after its own image" (Marx and Engels "Communist Manifesto" 13).

Let us begin the present section with a terse recapitulation of our position. We acknowledge that we presently, in the year 2017, live under capitalism. Capitalism, primarily, is the system in which man's economic relations are organized in such a way as to privilege a specific, and dominant, social class—the bourgeoisie. And this system lies upon two foundational characteristics: exploitation and alienation. We acknowledge that, while many previous epochs of history have utilized an exploitative social class structure in one way or another, the uniqueness of our time lies upon the lynchpin of globalism in regards to capitalism. Where the bourgeoisies, as a class, rose specifically from the culture of feudalism, manorialism, and the dark ages of Europe, we can now find them everywhere as the dominant social class—entrenched in all corners of the globe, in all nations. Via the wave of European revolutions against the nobilities, the bourgeoisies here rose to power in France, there in the Americas. And it was in the Americas where bourgeois capitalism took deepest root.

As a nation founded upon mercantile capitalism, the United States quickly positioned itself as the bourgeois nation par excellence, dominating the globe through a series of wars without end, strict economic controls, and aggressive geopolitical strategizing. Of its 241 years of existence as a sovereign nation, the U.S. has been at war for 224— in some form or another. This equates to military action for 92.9% of the overall lifespan of the United States. Zoltan Grossman, in his article "From Wounded Knee to Syria: A Century of U.S. Military Interventions," demonstrates how the U.S. has known fewer than *ten years of peace* in the past hundred. From this, it is safe to assert that as the heart of now-global bourgeois capitalism, the U.S. is an aggressor nation to its core, predicating, as it does, upon warfare without end. And from this we can also safely assert that U.S.-locus capitalism itself—the now-dominant mode of global production—is an aggressor system, also predicating upon war. We can demonstrate this with a simple Barbara (AAA-1) syllogism:

1. The central locus of present-day capitalism lies within the U.S.
2. The U.S. is a warfare state
3. Thus present-day capitalism predicates upon U.S.-sanctioned warfare

Given the dominance of the globe by both the U.S. and U.S.-locus economy, we must begin to equate the socio-economic problems of the world with the productive mode under which it is presently existing, *and* with the nation which presently enacts such a mode: war deaths, starvation, homelessness, poverty, rampant environmental destruction for profit—all of these are symptomatic of both U.S. policy *and* the dominant mode of production. There is, however, one subsection of humanity who seem to avoid all of the negatives of capitalism. They are those for whom the economic system exists: the bourgeoisies.

We are not, here, engaging in gross reduction, nor useless blame, but are rather pinpointing the source of the great evil of our time. At the root of all happenings between men are men themselves. Warfare happens between men, starvation happens to men, homelessness happens to men, poverty happens to men, and environmental destruction is both meted out and suffered by men. All of the problems of our age thus emerge from and against humanity itself. But, we must remember that, "[c]apitalism is neither a person nor an institution. It neither wills nor chooses. It is a logic at work through a mode of production: a blind, obstinate logic of accumulation" (Beaud 129). And as such, we cannot place the blame upon the abstraction of such a logic, but upon this logic as it presents itself in the minds of men; we must place the blame squarely upon humanity itself. Yet we cannot place the blame for the aforementioned woes upon those who suffer their effects—we would not, for example, blame the earth itself for the damage upon it which we dole out. No, the problem here does not lie with the victim, but rather with the aggressor. And as such, the problem—this great evil—is not faceless.

We reassert here that our problem lies with man himself, but not man as a totality: our problem lies only with some men—the dominant social class of men. While we all, to some degree, are complicit in capitalism's blind logic of accumulation—all of us swimming in the base-legitimating ideology of the bourgeoisie—we must not, as the oppressed, internalize such a blame. Rather, we must place our blame squarely upon those who profit from such a system of destruction, of warfare, and of profit itself. We must blame the bourgeoisie class. Men and women die consistently, however. One problematic man will be dead in, at most, one hundred years. Our blame then, while it might be levied, presently, upon specific individuals, must, more accurately, fall upon the *ideological structure which legitimates the problematic class itself*: our blame must fall squarely upon bourgeois ideology—the legitimating, now-global ideology which props up and reproduces our bourgeoisie, generation after generation. Bourgeois ideology, entailing the specifically alienating bourgeois land relations, is the true locus of our blame; the target of our attack.

In the previous pages of our polemic, we have built our case as soundly as possible. We have explored the history of the bourgeoisie class, we have discussed the ways in which the endemic alienation of bourgeois ideology has separated us, as a species-being, from our natural world context—a fundamental characteristic of what we are calling "bourgeois land relations"—and we have discussed the ways in which bourgeois ideology has coopted our reason, subverted our intentions, and how it enacts itself most effortlessly as a tool of social control—what we have called the "machine of civil society." We have discussed how bourgeois ideology is both produced and reproduced via public education, and we have suggested that education—radical education—itself is a primary avenue for revolution against bourgeois ideology and against capitalism at large. And we have discussed three preconditional necessities for a new articulation of communistic land relations. We have discussed how a salvific communism *must* be critical. We have discussed the necessity of a *political* focus in regards to communist land relations—our mental enslavement under bourgeois ideology being a political violation deserving of nothing less than *political* attention. And finally, we have discussed how a theory of communist land relations must be dialectical; it must emerge from a conception of reality that recognizes the illusion—the abstracted emptiness of language—and acknowledges the sublated, tensioned unity of all oppositions. In these regards, the philosophical lenses of both Marx and Wittgenstein are of the utmost importance.

Following all of this, where now should we turn? We assert that in the fight against capitalism, a remembrance of the historical struggle must not be abandoned. As long as there has been capitalism, there have been those who have rejected it; those who have fought it. Bourgeois ideology would have us believe that there is no alternative to global capitalism, to bourgeois class rule. We must not be misled. There are still pockets of socialism, of communist intentions, in our world—whether in the form of small communal societies or large nation-states such as China, Cuba, Vietnam, and Laos. And these pockets must be continually looked to, aligned with, critiqued, and supported. From Kant to Rousseau, Marx to Marcuse, the history of communistic opposition is long and rich. And it must never be forgotten. It must be leaned upon and it must be continually rekindled if we are ever to see a world in which all (wo)men are held to be truly equal—a world in which the eradication of class society, the eradication of the profit motive, and the eradication of all social oppressions follow most naturally from a ubiquitously beneficial socio-economic formation; our earth finally viewed as the *only* viable habitat for life as we know it. We must look to the great history of the communist theorists, the communist and socialist societies, and we must ground our work within the soil which they have tilled. We are the last of the hominins—the last species of a once diverse genus. And we have an opportunity to either accept what bourgeois ideology would have us believe is our fate—a total submission to a global capitalism which is systematically poisoning and destroying our world and all life—or fight. And we should fight. Complicity in this case is fatalistic.

CITATIONS

Adorno, Theodor. "Commitment." *The Essential Frankfurt School Reader*, edited by
     Andrew Arato and Eike Gebhardt, Continuum, 1987, pp. 300 –
319.

---. "Freudian Theory and the Pattern of Fascist Propaganda." *The Essential Frankfurt
     School Reader*, edited by Andrew Arato and Eike Gebhardt, Continuum, 1987, pp.
118 – 138.

---. "On the Fetish Character in Music and the Regression of Listening." *The Essential
     Frankfurt School Reader*, edited by Andrew Arato and Eike Gebhardt, Continuum,
1987, pp. 270 – 300.

---. "The Sociology of Knowledge and Its Consciousness." *The Essential Frankfurt School
     Reader*, edited by Andrew Arato and Eike Gebhardt, Continuum, 1987, pp. 452 –
466.

---. "Subject and Object." *The Essential Frankfurt School Reader*, edited by Andrew Arato
     and Eike Gebhardt, Continuum, 1987, pp. 497 – 512.

Althusser, Louis. *On the Reproduction of Capitalism: Ideology and Ideological State Apparatuses.*
     Verso, 2014.

Arato, Andrew, and Eike Gebhardt, eds. *The Essential Frankfurt School Reader.* Continuum,
     1987.

Arendt, Hannah. *Eichmann in Jerusalem: A Report on the Banality of Evil.* Penguin Books,
     1963.

Ariew, Roger, and Eric Watkins, eds. *Modern Philosophy: An Anthology of Primary Sources.*
     Hackett Publishing Company, 2009.

Beaud, Michel. *A History of Capitalism: 1500-2000*. Monthly Review Press, 1981.

Benjamin, Walter. *The Work of Art in the Age of Mechanical Reproduction*. Prism Key Press,
	2010.

---. "The Author as Producer." *The Essential Frankfurt School Reader*, edited by Andrew
	Arato and Eike Gebhardt, Continuum, 1987, pp. 254 – 270.

Egner, Robert, and Lestor Dennon, eds. *The Basic Writings of Bertrand Russell: 1903 –
	1959*. Routledge, 1992.

Freire, Paulo. *Pedagogy of the Oppressed*. Bloomsbury, 2000.

Freud, Sigmund. *Introductory Lectures on Psycho-Analysis*. Liveright, 1989.

Godwin, William. *An Enquiry Concerning Political Justice, and its Influence on General Virtue and
	Happiness*. Robinson, 1793. files.libertyfund.org/files/90/0164-01_Bk.pdf.
	Accessed 13 April 2017.

Gross, Bertram. *Friendly Fascism*. South End Press, 1980.

Grossman, Zoltan. "From Wounded Knee to Syria: A Century of U.S. Military
	Interventions."
academic.evergreen.edu/g/grossmaz/interventions.html.
	Accessed 13 April 2017.

Habermas, Jürgen. *The Structural Transformation of the Public Sphere: An Inquiry into a
	Category of Bourgeois Society*. Trans. Thomas Burger. MIT Press, 1989.

Heidegger, Martin. "The Origin of the Work of Art." *Off the Beaten Track*, edited by
	Julian Young and Kenneth Haynes, Cambridge, 2002, pp. 1 – 56.

Hoare, Quintin, and Geoffrey Smith, eds. *Selections from the Prison Notebooks of Antonio
	Gramsci*. International Publishers, 1999.

hooks, bell. *Teaching Community: A Pedagogy of Hope*. Routledge, 2003.

---. *Teaching Critical Thinking: Practical Wisdom*. Routledge, 2010. Print.

---. *Teaching to Transgress: Education as the Practice of Freedom*. Routledge, 1994.

Horkheimer, Max. "The Authoritarian State." *The Essential Frankfurt School Reader*, edited
	by Andrew Arato and Eike Gebhardt, Continuum, 1987, pp. 95 – 118.

---. "The End of Reason." *The Essential Frankfurt School Reader*, edited by Andrew Arato
        and Eike Gebhardt, Continuum, 1987, pp. 26 – 49.
---. "On the Problem of Truth." *The Essential Frankfurt School Reader*, edited by Andrew
        Arato and Eike Gebhardt, Continuum, 1987, pp. 407 – 444.
Hume, David. "An Enquiry Concerning Human Understanding." *Modern Philosophy: An*
        Anthology of Primary Sources, edited by Roger Ariew and Eric Watkins, Hackett,
        2009, pp. 533 – 601.
Kant, Immanuel. *Political Writings*. Cambridge, 2008.
Kirchheimer, Otto. "Changes in the Structure of Political Compromise." *The Essential*
        Frankfurt School Reader, edited by Andrew Arato and Eike Gebhardt, Continuum,
        1987, pp. 49 – 71.
Lenin, V.I. "The State and Revolution." *Essential Works of Lenin: What is to be Done? And*
        Other Writings, edited by Henry Christman, Dover, 1966, pp. 271 - 364.
Lukács, Georg. *History and Class Consciousness: Studies in Marxist Dialectics*.
        The MIT Press, 1968.
Marcuse, Herbert. *An Essay on Liberation*. Boston: Beacon Press, 1969.
---. *One-Dimensional Man*. Boston: Beacon Press, 1964.
Marx, Karl, and Friedrich Engels. *Capital Volume I*. Trans. B. Fawkes. Penguin Classics,
        1990.
---. *The Communist Manifesto*. International Publishers, 2016.
---. *Early Writings*. Trans. E.B. Bottomore. McGraw-Hill, 1964.
---. *The German Ideology: Parts I & III*. Martino Publishing, 2011.
---. *The Holy Family: Critique of Critical Critique*. Foreign Languages Publishing House,
        1956.
Mehic, Dino. "How Capitalism Influences Our Morality." *Hectic Dialectics*.
        hecticdialectics.com/2014/01/20/how-capitalism-influences-our-morality/.
        Accessed 13 April 2017.
Moore, Matthew. "Wittgenstein, Value Pluralism and Politics." *Philosophy & Social*

Criticism, 1 November 2010, pp. 1113 – 1136.

Parsons, Lucy. *Freedom, Equality, and Solidarity: Writings and Speeches 1878 –
1937*. Kerr,
> 2004.

Rahbaran, Shiva. *The Paradox of Freedom: A Study of the Life and Writing of
Nicholas Mosley*.
> Dalkey Archive Press, 2007.

Stern, David. Review of *Marx and Wittgenstein: Knowledge, Morality and
Politics*, by Gavin
> Kitching and Nigel Pleasants, eds. *Notre Dame Philosophical Reviews*,
2015.
> ndpr.nd.edu/news/marx-and-wittgenstein-knowledge-morality-
> and-politics/. Accessed 13 April 2017.

Tlumak, Jeffrey, ed. *Classical Modern Philosophy: A Contemporary Introduction*.
Routledge,
> 2007.

Warren, Scott. *The Emergence of Dialectical Theory*. The University of Chicago
Press, 1984.

Wittgenstein, Ludwig. *Tractatus Logico-Philosophicus*. Trans. C.K. Ogden.
Dover
> Publications, 1999.